TEXAS GRANITE

STORY OF A
WORLD WAR II HERO

Show me a hero and I will write you a tragedy.
Notebooks of F. Scott Fitzgerald

In loving memory to Jack Lummus

Library of Congress Cataloging-in-Publication Data
Hartman, Mary
   Texas granite : story of a World War II hero/Mary Hartman.
     p. cm.
   Includes bibliographical references and index.
   ISBN 1-885777-07-8 (acid free paper)
   1. Lummus, Jack, 1915-1945. 2. Iwo Jima, Battle of, 1945.
3. United States. Marine Corps—Biography. 4. Marines—United
States—Biography 5. Football players—United States—Biography.
I. Title
D767.99.I9H36   1996
940.54'26 — dc21   96-39051
                                        CIP

©1997 by Mary S. Hartman
Cover Design by Jared Wilson/ Dallas
Book Design by Intentions Graphic Design/ Dallas
5, 4, 3, 2, 1

Quotation from the *Notebooks of F. Scott Fitzgerald* reprinted by permission Harold
Ober Associated, Inc.

Frontispiece: Photograph of Jack Lummus taken upon graduation from Officers
Candidate School at Quantico, Virginia, on December 30, 1942. (Courtesy U. S. Marine
Corps Historical Branch)

Hendrick-Long Publishing Company
Dallas, Texas 75225-1123

CONTENTS

A Message to the Reader

This is a story about a man, a hero. His name was Jack Lummus, and he came from Ennis, a small town in central Texas.

On December 7, 1941, when the Japanese bombed U. S. ships at Pearl Harbor, Jack gave up a promising career as an end with the New York Giants professional football team. He enlisted in the United States Marines as a private. Before the war ended, he was a first lieutenant and had earned the nation's highest military award: the Medal of Honor.

I met Jack when I moved to Hollywood, California, from my hometown in Nebraska. During the next several months, we danced to swing bands, swam in the Pacific Ocean, and fell in love.

By the time the Fifth Marine Division took Jack off to fight the Japanese on Iwo Jima, we had agreed to marry when he came home.

Then enemy snipers in three separate pillboxes pinned down the men of his platoon. Jack ran out and single-handedly silenced their weapons. He survived that but then he stepped on a land mine. He didn't survive that blast.

This is the story of a young Texas boy whose brave deeds made all America proud of him. This is the story of Jack Lummus, just like genuine Texas granite, a genuine Texas hero.

CHAPTER ONE

BIG MAN ON CAMPUS

Big Jack Lummus felt as proud as the chief rooster in a hen house when he and his son-in-law, Tommy Merritt, drove out of Ennis that early-September morning in 1937. Riding along on the 67-mile trip to Waco were his son Jack and another Ennis, Texas, boy, both on their way to register at Baylor University.

Halfway there, Big Jack parked the Chevrolet at a Hillsboro restaurant and took the boys to lunch. He ordered a grilled cheese sandwich.

"Bring me a glass of beer to wash it down," he told the waitress. Then he turned to Jack. "You're legal drinking age by now, son. Have a beer with your old man."

Jack shook his head. "No, thanks, Dad. We're practically there." Once Jack stepped foot on the Baylor campus he would consider himself in training for the football

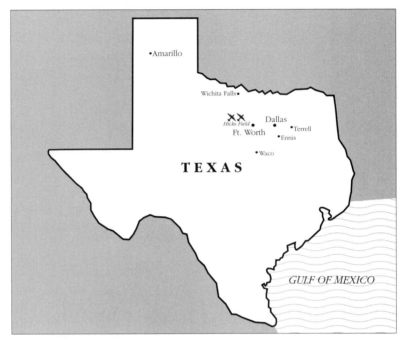

squad. He didn't want to turn up with beer on his breath and jeopardize his scholarship. Besides, alcohol had caused friction between his father and mother, and Jack didn't want to make it any easier for his dad to drink.

Big Jack worked as Ennis' night constable. Everyone in town liked and respected him, although many knew that Big Jack drank more than he should have. Some folks blamed it on his sorrow at losing the cotton farm.

But during the Depression, when almost half of the nation's workers stood in breadlines or rode boxcars, looking for jobs, Big Jack hadn't been able to find work, either. All three kids had pitched in and worked, but it hurt Big Jack's pride to see Laura making do on what

Jack and his sisters, Thelma and Sue, brought home. The Lummus family wasn't in any different a predicament from nearly every other family in the nation. But they had pulled together and always managed to have good food to eat. Besides, they had each other and had fun together. Even after their daddy joined the police force, the children still put their earnings into the sugar bowl for rent and groceries and school clothes.

When the group finished lunch that September day, Big Jack drove on to Waco and helped his son get settled into his dormitory. By the time his father and Tommy started back to Ennis, Jack had enrolled, choosing his-

Jack Lummus as a student at Ennis High School, Ennis, Texas. (Courtesy Sue Merritt)

tory as his major course of study. Soon he was on the football field, eager to try out for the varsity team.

During those early scrimmages, Jack played as he had the previous two years at Texas Military College in Terrell. Jack's former high school coach, Zebbie Howell, had recruited him to play for the school. As athletic director, Howell was able to offer Jack a scholarship even though

Building on the campus of Texas Military College, Terrell, Texas. The top floor was the dormitory where Jack Lummus lived for two years while attending the school. (Courtesy Jack Black)

Jack Lummus, left, and the other four were all on football scholarships at Texas Military College. The others are, (left to right), Louis Robinson, Jack Black, Bobby Taylor, and Willie Williams. After two years at TMC, all five entered Baylor University on football scholarships. (Courtesy Jack Black)

Jack had dropped out of high school. Howell figured Jack would have considered graduation expenses, such as a cap and gown, a class picture, or a yearbook, frivolous. Howell knew about the Lummuses' financial situation and knew the boy had been too proud to admit that he couldn't, or wouldn't, waste his family's scarce resources. He also knew it would be a terrible waste if young Jack Lummus threw away his magnificent athletic talents.

Jack's effortless runs down the field to snag passes caught the eye of Baylor coach Morley Jennings. When the day came for the Baylor Bears to suit up for their initial game, Jennings started Jack as first-string end. For the next four years, Jack wore green-and-gold jersey number 53.

"You'd think he wasn't mean enough to play football," said Jack Black, another athlete who had won a Baylor scholarship at Texas Military. In the dorm or at the malt shop, Jack was easygoing and hard to anger. "But when things got rough on the football field," Black said, "he had a different personality. He would knock an opponent's block off." Jack displayed his competitive side when he got into a fist fight with a Texas Christian University player during a hotly contested game.

The TCU game took place in Fort Worth. For a boy who had grown up on a central-Texas cotton farm, new vistas opened up on those train rides to play other Texas colleges. The team even went to Denver and played an injury-riddled game. They traveled clear out to Los Angeles for a game with Loyola, ranked the nation's best team that year.

Tommy and Sue Merritt lived in the Los Angeles area by then. They cheered when Jack caught a midfield pass and carried the ball a dazzling 45 yards for a touchdown.

"What a great day for Jack Lummus!" shouted the announcer. "His sister is in the grandstand, and he's especially proud to have scored."

One wintry Saturday, Jack and his teammates journeyed to Lincoln, Nebraska, for a game against the Nebraska Cornhuskers. I happened to be at the university myself that day for a high school journalism conference. The sponsors gave us passes to the game. I sat in the grandstand among a handful of fans, watching the Cornhuskers battle the Bears. I had dressed for a school conference, not a blizzard. By half-time, my silk-clad legs seemed to be turning blue. I left. I didn't know that the tall gangly boy trying to catch passes down there on the slippery field would one day capture my heart.

Had I read the sports pages of the *Omaha World-Herald*, I might have learned that a Texas sportswriter called that Baylor end "a great offensive performer who can snag overhead pegs with the best of them." Those in sports circles expected Jack Lummus to turn professional after college, for he'd already won several honors. His first year on Baylor's team, he made honorable mention on the All-Southwest Conference football team. On Christmas Day of 1940, he was a starting end when the conference's All-Stars played in San Antonio. Rehashing that game, a sportswriter described him as "tall and brilliant." An Associated Press reporter marveled at the "sensational leap the great pass receiver, Lummus, made on the goal line to gather in the throw for the fifth score."

Jack's fame spread beyond Texas. Two years in a row, Associated Press sportswriters nominated him to the All-American team. Just being nominated was almost reward enough, but in 1938 Jack made the honorable mention list.

As brilliantly as Jack played on the gridiron, many thought his most dynamic game was baseball. When he showed up for baseball practice that

Jack Lummus as an end for the Baylor University Bears, 1937-41. (*Courtesy* Texas Collection, Baylor University, Waco, Texas)

first spring of 1938, Coach Lloyd Russell watched him grab flies on the run and sock balls out of the ballpark. He saw a young man with "great speed, great hands, great determination." For the next four years, Jack played centerfield on Baylor's baseball team where his height helped him snag flies but never got in the way of his agility and speed.

"I can still see him in motion," said Harry Tennison, the team's third baseman and relief pitcher. "He had those graceful movements that some great athletes have—so smooth they're deceptive."

Teammate Travis Nelson agreed. "He could cover more ground than a six-inch snowstorm." Nelson said Coach Russell would play the left fielder on the left base line, the right fielder on the right line, and tell Jack to cover everything in between. "He'd amaze me," Nelson said. "He was always able to get to the ball, no matter how far he had to go." Jack's long legs helped, he said, but his great determination was what made the difference.

Jack's spectacular catches made him famous among Texas baseball fans. Often a batter socked a ball into one of the giant oak trees that grew behind centerfield. Jack would wait under the tree, follow the ball from limb to limb, and make the catch that put the batter out.

Fans still talk about Baylor's game with the University of Texas and the frustration Jack dished out to UT's batters. Harry Tennison was pitching his fast ball. "Cra-a-ck" went the bats. Three times in a row, Longhorn batters sent what appeared to be sure-fire homeruns sailing deep in centerfield. Three times Jack leaped high and snagged the balls. He retired the side. When Texas came up the next inning, Jack again palmed the first two balls. Then UT's star long-ball hitter, Pete Layden, came to bat. Aware that Layden usually pulled to the right, Jack trotted over to right field. This time, though, Layden hit the ball straight to center. Jack ran like a gazelle, stretched out the full length of his long frame, and one-handed the ball. The crowd went wild. Baylor fans who saw that game called it

"The Catch."

Shagging flies wasn't Jack's only talent. During his four years with the Bears, he maintained a .320 batting average; but long before he came to Baylor, he had a well-deserved reputation for hitting home runs. The first day he went out for football scrimmage, a new teammate ran up.

"I'd know this long, tall drink of water anywhere," he said, shaking hands and giving his name: Jack Willis from Flint, Texas. "I remember when our town team played your team at Ennis one Sunday afternoon. I can still see the homerun you hit that day. It sailed out of the park and all the way down the street into a lady's front yard."

It didn't surprise baseball fans when Jack earned the All-Southwest Conference centerfielder title three years running—1938, 1939, and 1940. It meant more to Jack, however, when Coach Russell told a reporter, "Jack Lummus is the greatest centerfielder in Baylor history—or anywhere else."

The future looked so bright that at times Jack felt like pinching himself. He could do anything he wanted. He changed his major to physical education so he could become a high school coach after he graduated. He considered a professional career in either football or baseball. He owed it all to Zebbie Howell. If he hadn't followed Zebbie to Texas Military, he'd never have made it to Baylor.

Playing on Baylor's varsity squads had many advantages, but one of the happiest for Jack was the food in the athlete's dining hall. For the first time in his memory, Jack could eat as much fried chicken and mashed potatoes and cream gravy as he wanted. Everything was plentiful. The serving bowls were filled and emptied and filled again. No one reminded Jack, as they often did at home, to go easy on the drumsticks, to save a thigh for his dad or a sister. Jack Willis marveled that no matter how many helpings of roast beef and fresh corn and yeast rolls Jack shoveled in, he never got fat; he stayed trim. By then he stood 6 foot 4 and weighed 194 pounds.

Jack studied, but he took time out for fun. He acted as unofficial "cheerleader" at basketball games. He instigated impromptu touch football games out behind the dormitory. When he and teammate Bob Nelson rented an off-campus apartment, it became the gathering place for athletes and other classmates.

If anybody had taken a popularity poll, Jack would have ranked near the top. He made friends with students from all over the campus. He dated many different girls but especially cared for one. She was strikingly beautiful and tall enough that she and Jack made a stunning pair on the dance floor. Sue Merritt suspected that she dealt Jack his first heartbreak. Sue couldn't be certain because Jack was such a proud, private person. He confided in no one and kept his innermost thoughts and feelings, especially his disappointments, locked inside himself.

Sue was visiting their folks when Jack came home for a weekend. A letter addressed to him arrived in the mail, and he picked it up and opened it. Sue watched him read and saw his expression plunge from anticipation to despair.

"He threw the letter down on the table," Sue said, "like it made him real mad. He spun around and stomped outside." Curious to know what had upset her brother, Sue picked up the letter and skimmed the first page. "It was a 'Dear John' letter—some girl giving him the gate."

Jack cooled off a bit and came back in. Sue tried to comfort him. "Don't worry about her," she said. "There are lots of girls around who'd be proud to go out with you."

"Sis, you mind your business, and I'll mind mine," Jack replied. Sue knew her brother well enough not to pursue the matter. "Jack didn't do much excess talking," she said. "He told you something once, and you'd better listen because that was it. When he *did* tell you something, you could believe it because his word was as good as gold."

Weekend visits home were rare, however, because of Jack's schedules. Football and baseball games took up most weekends. Jack also took odd jobs to help pay his way through school. During the school year, he delivered laundry and dry cleaning to dorm students. In summer, he and some of Texas' best college athletes dug ditches for the Atlantic Pipe Line Company. He made 65 cents an hour for backbreaking labor that we do today with backhoes. The company headquartered Jack's crew in eastern Texas near Beaumont.

Jack's last year in college was 1941. By then, the world war raging across Europe occupied all our minds. A military draft had been imposed the previous year, and all young men between the ages of 21 and 36 had registered for the Army. Many had already been called up or had enlisted in the Navy or Marines.

On May 26, 1941, an Army Air Corps recruiter visited Baylor's campus. Along with 25 other young men, mostly football players, Jack enlisted in a civilian flying school. He passed his physical. Then while he waited to be called up, he dropped out of school. Neither his family nor school officials know why he didn't stay in school long enough to get his degree. Grades weren't the reason; a check of his school transcripts showed that he carried a satisfactory grade average. More likely, Jack's defection had to do with the terrible turmoil the world faced. The Germans were bombing England and were about to invade Russia. America's congressmen argued for and against going to war. Jack's emotions, just like the emotions of every other young American, seesawed violently. Should he enlist in the Navy? In the Marines? Or should he sit on his hands and wait for the Army to draft him? Under any circumstance, he would have to put the rest of his life on hold until the world settled down. Even that cloud might have a silver lining. When the war ended, maybe he could come back and play another year of football.

CHAPTER TWO

FROM HOME RUNS TO AIRPLANES

In the first two months after Jack Lummus left Baylor University, he wore three different hats. First, he put on the baseball cap of a semiprofessional baseball player, then the garrison cap of an Air Corps cadet, and, finally, the helmet of an end with a professional football team.

The baseball uniform came his way when he signed on to play outfield with the Class D Spudders, a semiprofessional ball club from Wichita Falls, Texas. Jack spent a week at home visiting with his parents. Then on June 12, 1941, he took a train to Amarillo. There he caught up with the Spudders, who were on a nine-day road trip, going around the state to play other league teams.

The Spudders, organized earlier that spring, competed

in the West Texas-New Mexico League. The league included the Amarillo Gold Sox, Lamesa Lobos, Lubbock Hubbers, Borger Gassers, and Pampa Oilers, all in Texas, and the Clovis, New Mexico, Pioneers.

When Jack joined the Spudders, they were struggling against a losing streak. Then with a new pitcher on the mound and Jack covering right field, the tide turned. The Spudders moved up from sixth to fourth place in the league. In that first game, the Spudders beat Amarillo, 14-0. The following night, Jack hit a double. The next player at bat hit the ball, and Jack tore for home. The game ended with Wichita Falls beating Amarillo, 1-0. Jack's run was the only score of the entire game.

Sportswriters scratched their heads. Who was Lummus? They thumbed through newspaper "morgue" files, looking for stories about this unknown outfielder.

By the time the Spudders returned to Wichita Falls, the reporters had it all figured out. This was the same Lummus who made a name for himself at Baylor University, both in football and baseball. Digging up Jack's reputation as a centerfielder, one reporter suggested that Sammy Hale, the Spudders' manager, switch Jack. No other centerfielder, he said, could cover as much ground as Jack Lummus. "We don't know of a better ball hawk in Texas," he wrote, "and that includes all the Texas League players." Hale read the story, and from then on, put Jack in at centerfield as often as right field.

Jack was one happy fellow. For once, he played a game he loved and got paid for it.

The fans were happy, too. Attendance at the Spudders' home games grew. Seven thousand fans sometimes filled the bleachers at the home games. Jack was one of their favorite players. They nicknamed him "Cactus Jack" and stomped and clapped whenever he came up to bat.

Then on July 6, Jack's professional baseball career came to an abrupt halt. Jack played his 26th game for the Spudders that night. It was his last game with the team. The Army Air Corps had notified Jack that he had to report to Hicks Field, 40 miles northwest of Fort Worth. The Air Corps expected Jack to honor the enlistment he had signed at Baylor. After the ninth inning, Jack went to his room and packed his bag. He took the night train to Fort Worth.

Jack and the other Baylor enlistees crowded into an Army bus. At Hicks Field, they moved into a cot-lined Quonset hut. The quartermaster issued them khaki uniforms with wings and vertical propellers appliqued on the pockets. The uniforms resembled the khakis worn by Army officers. However, until they passed all their flying tests and graduated, they would not be considered officers. Neither would they be considered enlisted men. They would simply retain the status of aviation flight cadets. Their superiors made sure they knew their place. They called them "dodos," large, extinct birds whose wings were useless for flying.

Except for the Baylor contingent, most of the cadets had enlisted at universities located in the southern and

Fairchild PT-19 trainer on the flight line at Hicks Field near Fort Worth, Texas, where Jack Lummus underwent pilot's training in the 1941 civilian Air Corps. (Courtesy Hal Harle, Waco, Texas)

eastern states. Most were gifted athletes. Jack looked forward to organizing some rousing football scrimmages with them. The instructors, however, kept the cadets so busy that they hadn't time for anything other than a few touch football games.

The Army Air Corps licensed the flight school but contracted out the operation to a civilian. Civilian pilots taught the courses. When the students learned to fly the single-wing Fairchild P-19 trainer planes, they received their wings and became second lieutenants in the Air Corps.

That summer of 1941 was a confusing time for all young people. Europe had gone to war in 1939 when Germany invaded Poland. In the two years since then, Germany had also marched into France, Denmark,

Norway, the Netherlands, Belgium, Greece, and Yugoslavia. The war spread beyond Europe when Italy joined forces with Germany and mounted an offensive in North Africa. Then in June of 1941, German troops stormed across the border into Russia.

After conquering Russia, Germany intended to cross the English Channel and occupy England. To soften British resistance, the Germans dropped bombs on London every night. Londoners evacuated their children to the countryside. Some British parents even sent their children across the Atlantic Ocean to live with strangers in America. Ships carrying those children risked sinking by German submarines.

Rumors began to spread about Adolph Hitler's imprisoning Jews and Gypsies and mentally deficient individuals in concentration camps. Refugees flooded British and American embassies, seeking asylum.

Debate went on all across the United States. Some of the people still remembered that Americans went to France to fight for peace in 1918. They blocked President Franklin Roosevelt's attempts to declare war on Germany and called themselves "isolationists." The president got around that by signing into law the Lend-Lease bill, which allowed America to loan ships and ammunition to U. S. Allies in Europe.

Confused young men registered for the draft but went on with their lives while they waited for the Army to call them into service. Young women kissed their friends goodbye when they joined the Army or Navy. Someone I knew went to Canada and enlisted in the Royal Canadian Air Force. I was looking forward to my junior year in high school. Little did I know that in the next two years there would be fewer and fewer boys in my classrooms. Instead of making phone calls, they would write lonesome letters from camps or ships.

Muddling Jack Lummus' mind even more were the phone calls that reached him at Hicks Field. The caller, a scout for the New York Giants football squad, called nearly every night. By mid-August, football practice for the fall season would be in full swing.

"Come on up to Wisconsin, Jack," coaxed the scout, "and work out with the best pro football team in the United States." As the scout's calls became more insistent, the pressure in flight school became tougher. Soon it would be time to go up for his first solo flight, and Jack didn't know what to do.

From news reports, it sounded as if the United States would enter the war in Europe any day. Jack felt a great obligation to serve his country. On the other hand, he didn't believe he had the strength to turn down a chance to play football with the New York Giants.

Finally the day came. Jack got in his Fairchild P-19, took off, and flew the required pattern. He made a perfect landing. Then he ran the tip of a wing into a fence.

That accident washed Jack out of cadet training. Because he was a civilian flight cadet, he had the option of going home or transferring to another branch of service.

Within a day or two, Jack Lummus was on a train,

heading for Wisconsin and his big break, a chance to show the coaches of the New York Giants what he could do.

CHAPTER THREE

LIFE AS A GIANT

Jack Lummus rode the train for three days, going from Dallas, Texas, almost to Canada. His ticket read "Superior, Wisconsin," a town on the southwestern tip of Lake Superior.

He felt like a stranger, so far from home. The farther north the train took him, the more foreign the language sounded. His fellow passengers rushed their sentences and ran words together in abrupt phrases. He had to ask nearly everyone to repeat what they had said.

Jack himself struck the Northerners as alien. Other travelers gawked at the tall, lanky young man. They stared at his ruddy complexion. They listened to his soft, slow drawl. Whenever he walked into a depot restaurant, waitresses argued over the privilege of taking his order.

They wanted to hear the Texan ask for "frahed okry."

When he arrived at Superior, the north woods and the lake shore looked like the terrain of a foreign country to him. Everything was so different from the flat, dry Texas plains where he had grown up.

Jack wasted no time. He suited up and ran onto the practice field with the others who were working out with the New York Giants. He read the roster of his teammates, and his jaw dropped in amazement. The list read like a Who's Who of sports figures. It included some of the best players from the nation's finest universities.

He began to feel more at home when he heard the soft, familiar accents of the other ends. Jim Poole had played for Mississippi State. Will Walls was an end from Texas Christian University. There was Jim Lee Howell, an Arkansan, who became Jack's close friend. Howell would come back in 1946 and coach the Giants to many outstanding victories. There also was a former player from Southern Methodist University and another from the Texas Aggies. But the biggest surprise of all was Bill Edwards, a tackler from Baylor.

During the rigorous practice sessions, Jack sweated and grunted and tackled sawdust dummies. He jogged to increase his speed and did calisthenics to build his muscle. He learned to take punishment and dish it out, too.

Steve Owen, the coach, kept a sharp eye out for top-notch players he would want to hire for the 1941 Giants season. Fewer than 50 would go to New York with the Giants that fall. Competition was hot and heavy.

Aerial view of the Polo Grounds in New York City where Jack Lummus spent the happiest four months of his life as a rookie end for the New York Football Giants. (*Courtesy New York Football Giants*)

Jack and the other candidates on the Superior gridiron didn't realize that the patterns they established would persist into the 21st century. Players still compete for slots on the professional teams. That much hasn't changed.

However, professional football was quite new then. When Jack started out, pro football was a young sport. The Giants were a young team. In 1925, a businessman named Tim Mara bought a football franchise for $2,500. He located the team at the Polo Grounds and called them the New York Giants. Nine years later, he turned the Giants over to his sons, Wellington and Jack. They hired Steve Owen of Phillips University as coach.

Owen became famous for a game he coached against the Giants' bitter rivals, the Chicago Bears. It was freezing that day, and the players' cleats slid on frozen ground. By half time, the Bears were leading, 10-3. Owen sent a locker room attendant out to beg, borrow, or buy as many tennis shoes as he could find. When play resumed, all the Giants wore sneakers. Owen had figured correctly. His team got better traction from their rubber soles than the Bears did with their cleats. The Bears' coach was furious. "Step on their toes," he ordered his players. Even so, the Giants won the game, 30-13. That game became known as the "Sneakers Game."

Owen was still coach when Jack arrived. Just before Labor Day, he culled out the weaker players. Jack Lummus was one of the 48 survivors who boarded the train for New York.

Jack still had hurdles to clear, though. Fifteen more players had to be cut from the roster before the Giants could begin playing regulation games. First, however, the Giants would see how well they fared in an exhibition game against the nation's best college athletes.

Opening ceremonies for the game with the College All-Stars started at 8:30 the night after the Giants arrived in New York. Jack ran onto the field, as he had hundreds of times for games at Waco, Texas. But this time his knees started knocking. Fifty-four thousand rowdy fans filled the bleachers. The crowd was 10 times larger than at any Baylor game. They cheered 10 times louder, too, when the Seventh Regiment band marched onto the field. Sailors from the British Navy followed. Then came midshipmen from the USS *Prairie State* and soldiers from nearby Army bases. Behind them strutted the U.S. Military Academy band and a battalion of gray-uniformed West Point cadets. Then Jack got goose bumps when the famous Army football squad paraded in.

The game began. Jack squatted on the Giants bench and mentally pinched himself. Half of him was afraid Coach Owen would forget to send him in. The other half was afraid he *wouldn't* forget. Jack had stage fright.

Even if Jack didn't feel like a member of the team yet, he certainly looked like one. He wore a Giants' blue jersey, number 29, and buff-colored canvas pants. On his head was a sectioned leather helmet. On his feet he wore laced-up, ankle-high boots with screw-in rubber cleats. The only protective padding went across his chest and over his hips. Jack's 1941 uniform didn't even look like a second cousin to the uniforms pro footballers wear today. It weighed about 30 pounds less, too.

The rules of the game were also different in 1941. For example, the substitution rule required that a player remain in the game—playing both offense and defense—for an entire quarter. If an injury forced him to leave the field, he couldn't go back in until the next quarter. If he were hurt so badly that he couldn't go back in, a substitute could replace him. Otherwise, the team finished that quarter with 10 players instead of 11. Consequently, coaches favored players with enough stamina to play all 15 minutes of a quarter. Better still, they wanted men who could play the full 60 minutes. Coaches looked for prospects with guts and brains. They didn't offer contracts to the weak.

All during the first half, Jack Lummus sat on the bench, tense and anxious. Would Coach send him in? When the team trotted out of the locker room after half time, Owen motioned Jack onto the field. Jack had already strutted his stuff during practice sessions. Now his big chance had arrived. He would prove he had what it took to help win games. And that's just what he did. During the third quarter, Jack threw a key block that enabled the Giants' ball carrier to score. Owen left Jack in for the fourth quarter, and he made a first down only nine yards from the goal line.

Steve Owen liked what the tall, swift-running Texan showed him. Before long, the owners called Jack in the office and offered him a contract as a free agent. His salary would be $100 a month.

Jack moved into the Whitehall Hotel on 100th and Broadway. It was an apartment-type hotel that the Maras booked for the team. Jack paid $30 each month to share two rooms and a kitchenette with four other players.

Every morning, Jim Lee Howell and Jack and some of the other players crossed Broadway to the corner drugstore. They took turns paying three cents for the *New York Times.* While they drank their coffee, they read about the game they'd played the Sunday before. On Friday, they'd read about the game they would play the next Sunday. Around nine, Howell and Jack would climb into Howell's car and drive to the Blue Hill Country Club, one of their training fields.

Practice sessions started out with calisthenics and sprints. Then they tackled sawdust dummies, driving hard and hitting low with their shoulders. Every 10 minutes, Coach Owen blew his whistle, and everyone dropped what they were doing to run laps around the field. On rainy days, they sat inside the dungeon-like clubhouse, studying photographs of their games or movies of their opponents' games. Coach Owen lectured them on football theories or sketched new formations on a blackboard. Outside again, they practiced the changes Owen had introduced.

Back at the hotel, they showered and went out for supper, usually at a pizza parlor. For 35 cents, they ate a full dinner, dessert included.

When Jack felt flush, he would go downtown with other team members. He might take in a movie or stop in a nightclub and listen to a jazz band. Toward the end of the month, money got scarce. Then Jack and Jim Lee Howell would walk all over Harlem, sightseeing. Sometimes, they wandered around Manhattan Island's canyon-like streets that ran between skyscrapers 40 or 50 stories high. They stared in the glittery windows of department stores like Macy's or Saks Fifth Avenue. They watched chauffeurs with chow guard dogs help fur-wrapped women out of gleaming limousines. They inhaled the new-leather tang of pitcher's mitts in Abercrombie & Fitch, a famous sporting goods store.

New York City was a heady experience for a young man not long away from a Texas cotton field. Jack tried not to be obvious when he stared at the slim, elegant women on the streets of Manhattan. And he found it hard to act cool when the Maras introduced him to eager girls. Jack didn't often accept when fans invited him out for dinner. He hesitated because he was serious about his career as a professional athlete. Besides, the coach insisted on an 11 o'clock curfew. If a player missed bedcheck, he would get a lecture and a $20 fine. Miss it too often, and he could be fired.

Jack didn't take chances. He followed the rules, and he played football as well or better than he had ever played for Baylor. He ran like the wind, and he snagged footballs off clouds. Of the ends that played for the Giants in 1941, Jim Lee Howell considered Jack the best.

CHAPTER FOUR

A NEW WORLD

Jack Lummus often pinched himself during that fall of 1941. He hadn't known there was such a world as he lived in. At the Sunday games, he rubbed shoulders with footballers so famous that almost every fan in the country would recognize their names. The names of most of his teammates also were household words: Mel Hein, Tuffy Leemans, and Ward Cuff. Even rookies like Jack came fresh from winning seasons with the nation's best college teams. There was All-American George Franck; Frank Reagan of Pennsylvania University; and Lou DeFillipo, Len Eshmont and Vince Dennery, all from Fordham, to name a few.

Orville Tuttle, another All-American, was a former assistant coach for the University of Oklahoma. Jim

Howell called him "Mister Five-by-Five," because he was short and stocky. He had a pair of legs that looked as if they had forgotten to grow. Howell, who joined the Giants in 1937, the same year as Tuttle, didn't like Tuttle's constant chatter. "Hey, hey, look at this," Tutt would brag. Or he'd stand on the sidelines and holler, "Get up there. Gotta git 'em, the Indians are coming." Later, as a Marine officer in California, Tutt would become one of Jack's friends. He played an important role in my life, too.

Every other week or so, Jack packed his bag and boarded a train. He rode in special cars, ate nourishing meals, and traveled in style. The team went to play against teams in the National Football League's Eastern Division: the Washington Redskins, Philadelphia Eagles, Pittsburgh Steelers. The trains took him to Cleveland for games with the Rams and to Detroit to battle the Lions. But when the Giants played their hated rival, the Brooklyn Dodgers, they rode the streetcar.

When the team suited up and ran out on the field for a big game, Jack usually sat on the bench the first quarter. Then Coach Owen would send him in as second-string defensive end. Jack pitted his skills against the toughest, meanest, best football players in the entire nation. He chased runners up the field. He intercepted passes and outsmarted some of the sharpest quarterbacks in the United States, such as Slinging Sammy Baugh, whose name had often made headlines in the *Dallas Times Herald's* sports section.

Jack chased and caught so well that Wellington Mara

told a *New York Times* reporter he intended to offer rookie Jack Lummus another contract the next year.

The Giants did well, too. They won first place in the league's Eastern Division. To earn the NFL's 1941 title, the Giants would have to defeat whoever took the Western Division pennant. There seemed little doubt that the Western Division champions would be the Chicago Bears.

Coach Owen, however, had more to worry about that fall than the title. He faced a ticklish situation. The previous year, Congress had passed the Selective Service Act. The Act required unmarried men between the ages of 21 and 36 to register for military service.

Owen began to worry when two of his most promising players received "Greetings" from their hometown draft boards. The draft threatened to deplete the rosters of all professional football and baseball teams. Bob Feller was ready to serve his country, but he couldn't decide whether to enlist in the Army or Navy.

Most of the Giants were single. And most of the Giants were healthy enough to pass physical exams. That included Jack.

While Jack was building a reputation in New York, I was a high school senior in Holdrege, Nebraska. While Jack was wondering whether the Giants would win the NFL title, I was wondering what I would do after graduation. I might go to New York City, I thought, and land a glamorous job. That didn't excite me nearly as much as the thought of Bob Wilson asking me to the senior prom that spring.

Sometimes, in quiet moments, I tried to picture the boy who would one day sweep me off my feet. I didn't see any prospects among the boys I dated then. They seemed to regard me more as a buddy than a sweetheart. I spent little time with my books, for studying didn't interest me. The school building was only a convenient stage where I could sing or play music. I studied piano. I sang in a trio, a mixed octet, a glee club. I sang duets, but it would be years before I overcame a devastating case of stage fright and performed alone. When the music teacher scheduled me for a solo in the district music contest, I developed acute appendicitis and went in for surgery instead. Ever since eighth grade, I had held first chair in the orchestra's string bass section and had organized my own jazz combo. I would jitterbug as long as the Benny Goodman records spun.

My mother insisted that I take a two-year course in stenography. I argued with her, but, as usual, she won. She was right, of course. Those skills have helped me earn my living ever since. They helped me then, too. By the time I was a senior in high school, I had acquired five part-time jobs.

On December 7, 1941, I was working at one of those jobs. I sold tickets to people attending the Sunday movie matinee. My life changed that afternoon. It would never be the same again.

CHAPTER FIVE

PEARL HARBOR DAY

The north wind that Sunday afternoon was brisk and cold. Gusts blew hats off heads and snatched programs out of fists. Since daylight, football fans from all over Manhattan Island had been jamming into subways and buses. All headed in the same direction: north to the Polo Grounds at 157th Street and 8th Avenue.

As the hands of the stadium clock moved toward game time, the hubbub grew louder. Elevated trains thundered into Coogan's Bluff station. Shouting passengers jumped off and ran toward ticket booths. New York City's mounted police blew whistles and nudged the crowd into orderly lines. Concessionaires chanted and held up their wares: hot dogs wrapped in waxed paper, purple bottles of grape soda, miniature footballs stamped "Made in Japan."

Sixty-six large men bypassed the ticket kiosks. They skirted the crowds and headed for the athletes' gate. Guards, recognizing them, allowed them to pass into the stadium. Half of these men entered the New York Giants' locker room. The other half found their way into the visitors' quarters. As the hands of the clock ate up minutes, the excitement in the locker rooms grew. Loud voices resounded. Towels snapped at bare bottoms. Nervous fingers pulled on jerseys: red and silver for the Brooklyn Dodgers, blue for the Giants.

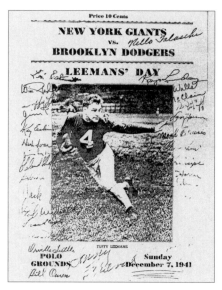

Jack Lummus was among the twenty-seven players signing the program of the Sunday, December 7, 1941, New York Giants vs. Brooklyn Dodgers football game. (Photocopy courtesy Stan Raytinsky)

The date was December 7, 1941. A battle would soon begin that New Yorkers had anticipated all year. It was the annual grudge match between the Brooklyn Dodgers and New York Giants. The victor would walk off with the coveted Metropolitan New York professional football title. To earn that title was a matter of fierce pride among Brooklynites and New Yorkers. Fist fights broke out when fans questioned a first down or objected to a referee's decision.

Dressed and raring to go, the teams trotted out to warm up on the field. Pregame ceremonies began, and the crowd found seats on the ice-cold cement bleachers. It was Tuffy Leemans Day. After Tuffy received his plaque and gifts, the audience quieted down for the national anthem. Then the Giants and Dodgers hurried back to their locker rooms for last-minute pep talks.

Behind the goal post, the hands on the clock stood at 1:50 P.M. Eastern Standard Time.

At that instant, a short-wave radio message was beaming into the Navy Department at Washington, D. C. The wire's shocking information would rupture the peace of all Americans. The message originated at the headquarters of Rear Adm. Husband E. Kimmel, commander-in-chief of the United States Pacific Fleet.

The admiral's cable read: "Air raid on Pearl Harbor. This is not a drill."

Fifteen minutes later, radio listeners, unaware of events taking place at Pearl Harbor, heard a hoarse roar. Both teams stormed onto the Polo Grounds, looking mean and ready to tangle.

During the first quarter, Jack Lummus sat on the bench with the second team. Used to mild Texas winters, he shivered in the cold December wind. The Dodgers made a first down on the Giants' four-yard line. The teams faced each other again, and the Dodgers forged their way to the three-yard line. Then they catapulted over the Giants' line for the first touchdown of the game.

Meanwhile, a flurry of activity broke out at the game in

Griffith Stadium, where the Washington Redskins were battling their visitors, the Philadelphia Eagles. Although the fans didn't know it, the excitement was a result of Admiral Kimmel's communique. The announcer turned on his microphone: "Call for Admiral Blanding." Then another message: "Major Butler, report to your office." And still another announcement. "Any employees of the *Washington Times-Herald* at the ballpark are asked to report to the newsroom." If fans became curious about those cryptic commands, their questions would remain unanswered for at least another half hour.

A courier carried a note to Edward A. Tamm's box at Griffith Stadium. Tamm was assistant to J. Edgar Hoover, director of the Federal Bureau of Investigation. The message center was holding a telephone call for Tamm. Patched into the connection was Hoover, in New York for the weekend. On the line was Robert L. Shivers, special FBI agent in charge of the Honolulu office. Shivers reported the chaos erupting around him. He held the phone out a window. Tamm and Hoover heard the explosions as Japanese fighter planes dive bombed American ships in the harbor. They heard the rat-a-tat-tat as Japanese nose guns strafed American planes on the airfields.

Unsuspecting fans at New York's Polo Grounds waited for a timeout to end and play to resume. They milled around, waved over hot dog vendors, headed for restrooms. Some stood to slap the heat of blood back into their gloved hands.

Half an hour into the Giants-Dodgers game, the Associated Press ticker machine up in the press box started chattering. A sports reporter wandered over to see what was coming out. The yellow tape carried the first-quarter score of the game going on at Chicago's Comiskey Park. "Cardinals 7, Bears 0." The teletype stuttered, hesitated, then started again. "Cut football running," read the purple block letters. Another pause, and then the bulletins began coming, one after the other. They came out so fast the operator didn't get a chance to paste them on forms.

"Airplanes identified as Japanese have attacked the American Naval Base at Pearl Harbor." Another message: "Order all military to return to bases."

The announcers at the New York and Washington games decided not to relay the shocking news over their microphones. Perhaps they were afraid people might panic. A stampede could break out and someone get hurt.

Then the devastating AP bulletins began to air over local radio stations. Eric Sevareid, a young announcer for a local New York station, broadcast hastily acquired details in his staccato style. In the Polo Grounds grandstands, fans carrying portable radios to keep tabs on other games, heard Sevareid's news. They spread the word.

Then Rush Holloway interrupted his radio broadcast of the Redskins game. Audiences from all over the United States heard him say, "Airplanes identified as Japanese have attacked the American Naval Base at Pearl Harbor. Stay tuned to this station for details."

From Maine to Southern California, the nation's citizens gasped in horror. They spun their radio dials in a frantic search for more of those details. Not many knew that Pearl Harbor was a huge American naval base near Honolulu. Those who did know undoubtedly had sons or husbands in the Navy. If their loved ones happened to be stationed in the Pacific, they wanted more details, and they wanted them *now*.

Americans hadn't realized that Japan presented a threat to our national interests. Why would the Japanese bomb our ships? they wondered. If any enemy were to attack us, it would surely be the German U-boats out in the Atlantic Ocean.

All across the country, families telephoned each other. What did you hear? they asked. Which radio station offers the latest news? Where on earth is Pearl Harbor? they wanted to know. From coast to coast, the Bell Telephone Company's lines buzzed with busy signals.

In downtown New York City, crowds stood in mute shock, staring at the Times Square Building. News bulletins rolled across electric lights high on the building's wall.

One of the bulletins announced that New York's Major Fiorello LaGuardia had summoned his emergency board to City Hall. He also ordered all off-duty policemen and firemen back on the job immediately.

At the Polo Grounds, tension crackled in the air like static electricity. On the playing field, however, the game plunged on. None of the players suspected anything amiss. They didn't notice servicemen leaving the grandstand in their olive drab and navy blue uniforms. They didn't question why the announcer croaked: "Attention please. Here is an urgent message. Will Col. William J. Donovan call Operator 19 in Washington immediately!" Neither Jack nor his teammates appreciated that the colonel was the White House's coordinator of information. In a few short months, Donovan would become chief of the Office of Strategic Services. Throughout the war, he would direct clandestine activities for President Franklin Delano Roosevelt.

The half ended and Jack and the other players shuffled off the field. Shouts rolled down from the grandstand. Excited fans waved their arms. Newsboys ran up the bleacher steps, waving "extra" editions of the New York papers.

Steve Owen followed the Giants into the steamy locker room. He had been up in the press box the last quarter. From that vantage point, he observed the Dodgers' tactics. Then he tossed down notes telling his team how to defend their lines. But he'd also heard about Pearl Harbor.

He didn't spend half time rehashing the secret plays he'd been drilling into his team during past weeks. Instead, he informed them about the Japanese attack. He told of enemy destroyers launching bombers off their decks. The planes flew on to Pearl Harbor and torpedoed our unwary naval ships. Luckily, some of the American fleet was out to sea, for the bombs sank or damaged nearly every ship anchored in Pearl Harbor. Japanese fighter planes flew over Hickam and Wheeler airfields. They strafed buildings and unloaded bombs on the airstrips. Air Corps planes were parked on the tarmac like ducks in a row. Before American pilots could jump in and get airborne, their planes went up in flames.

Where was Pearl Harbor? the stunned footballers asked. The Hawaiian Islands, Owen told them. At Oahu, offshore from Honolulu. Two thousand miles off America's West Coast. Too close for comfort to San Francisco and Los Angeles.

That was that, then. America was at war.

The attack depressed Coach Owen. He was about to lose most of his players. All the Giants' unmarried men would be called up. All would pass the physical. Their lives would be at risk. When his men went, his investment went, too: months of training, thousands of dollars, and a heart full of hope.

Coach Owen told reporters that some of his men had already talked to recruiters. Jack Lummus, he said, had visited a Navy recruitment center. Others planned to wait for their draft boards to drag them in. But that was before Pearl Harbor. An enemy had attacked the beloved country of red-blooded Americans. Their heartbeats quickened. They felt chills, not from the cold but from excitement. Like it or not, they faced the prospect of going off and becoming part of momentous events. Those events would change their lives forever.

Jack's glance fell on a poster nailed to the back wall. It was a drawing of a rugged-looking Marine, wearing a helmet and holding a rifle. Underneath the picture ran the message: "Want action? Join the U. S. Marine Corps."

All Jack knew about war was what he'd heard his uncle say about the Great War of 1918. The war to end all wars. And yet here came another war. A wild roller coaster of emotions swept over Jack. Some of it resembled fear. Fear, maybe, of the bombs and bullets the newsreels showed killing British commandos. Some of it felt like pride. Pride that his country needed him. He pictured himself in a snappy uniform, strolling down a boulevard with a sultry brunette on his arm. Marching through Paris. Coming home wearing rows of ribbons that marked all the battles he had fought in. Yes, it felt like fear, but most of all, it felt like excitement.

Jack prayed that the war wouldn't end before he could get into it. He yearned to dash out of the locker room and tear back to the hotel—pack his bag and jump into the red 1940 Ford coupe he had bought. He would break all speed limits and drive back to Texas. Then he would sign up.

But sadness swept over him. What about his big plans? he asked himself. His future had looked so bright that morning. Now he would have to postpone his football career for the next year or two. Maybe longer.

As if to remind Jack of the future within his grasp, Coach Owen sent him in at the third quarter. He finished out the game. As the sun sank toward the Hudson River, the struggle dragged on.

The news about Pearl Harbor threw a pall over everyone. The fans weren't in a mood to watch; the teams weren't in a mood to play. The Dodgers beat the Giants, 21 to 7.

Before the day ended, Americans started to consolidate their defense. President Roosevelt sat up late that night, composing the speech he would make the next day. "Yesterday, December 7, 1941," he wrote, "a date which will live in infamy, the United States of America was suddenly and deliberately attacked by naval and air forces of the Empire of Japan." He would end by asking Congress to declare the nation at war.

I sat up late myself, talking to Mother. One of my friends had stood in line that afternoon to buy a ticket for the movie.

"Did you hear what happened at Pearl Harbor?" she had asked.

CHAPTER SIX

UNCLE SAM WANTS *YOU*

Two weeks after the Japanese attacked America's fleet at Pearl Harbor, the New York Giants journeyed west for the title match with the Chicago Bears. The outcome of the December 21 game would decide which team clinched the 1941 National Football League title.

Sports reporters wrote dozens of columns about the coming game at the ivy-walled Wrigley Field. The contest would be a battle of champions, with the Bears as the league's Western Division champions and the Giants as the Eastern Division champions.

Although the Giants wouldn't admit it, their chances of winning looked slim. They arrived in Chicago with several players sidelined. Some were in bed with the flu. Others sat on the bench wearing bandages and casts, looking like refugees from a train wreck. During the Pearl Harbor Day game with the Dodgers, they had incurred broken noses, skin gashes, injured hips, and sprained ankles. Orville Tuttle's big toe was split.

Even if the Giants had been in top shape, the match still would have been an uphill battle. The Bears had played phenomenal ball during the 1941 season. They set seven records and managed to get Coach George Halas and six players inducted into the Pro Football Hall of Fame. Sportswriters still rank the 1941 Bears among the six best football squads in NFL history.

So it wasn't a surprise when the Bears tromped all over the Giants that Sunday afternoon.

For 10 minutes after kickoff, the Bears didn't let the Giants even get a whiff of what the ball smelled like. Then Tuffy Leemans shot George Franck a pass, and Franck raced 31 yards for a touchdown. The Bears blocked the extra point. By half time, the Bears had scored three field goals to lead 9 to 6. In the second half, the Giants made a field goal to tie the score. Then, as if the Bears smelled victory, they struck like a Sherman tank. They smothered Giants' plays, intercepted their passes, and chalked up three touchdowns. With nine seconds left in the game, the Bears faked a drop kick and ran 42 yards for a fourth touchdown.

Final score: Bears, 37, Giants, 9.

A sad Jack Lummus slumped off the field. The last professional football game he would play had turned into a rout. Worse, the Mutual Broadcasting System had aired the game coast-to-coast. Jack pictured his family down in Ennis, Texas, their ears glued to the receiver, their faces long because Jack's team got soundly whipped.

Adding insult to injury, Jack pocketed $288.70, his share of the money earned from tickets sold at the gate. He had anticipated receiving closer to a thousand dollars. Gate receipts for 1941 were the smallest for any playoff game in NFL history. Fewer than 13,000 fans had shown up at Wrigley Field that day. Americans stayed home, worried and confused. Gloomy news bulletins alarmed them even more. Three days before, the Japanese had attacked an American tanker off the California coast. On December 20, long-range enemy submarines again fired on two more American ships.

Back in New York, Jack packed his possessions into the trunk of his Ford. He slid under the steering wheel. Howie Yeager and Orville Tuttle crammed their oversized frames into the two-passenger coupe, and Jack turned the car's chrome grill south. He drove out of New York City.

The trio arrived in Ennis the Saturday after Christmas. They finished off the holiday turkey and ham that Jack's mother had cooked two days earlier. Famished for home cooking, the footballers demolished the sweet potato pudding and devoured Laura's famous light-bread rolls. After dinner, Jack took his nephew, Pete, outside and taught him to ride the new bike Santa had brought. Relatives stopped by to tell Jack "howdy" and shake hands with his celebrated guests.

On Sunday, Jack pored over the *Dallas Times Herald.*

The edition carried photographs of the devastation at Pearl Harbor. The capsized USS *Oklahoma* looked like a toppled elephant. Adrift in the murky waters of the bay, Jack saw the torn shells of eight battleships, three cruisers, and three destroyers. Partially submerged mine sweepers and other smaller vessels clogged the shipping lanes. Shots of the airfields showed the carcasses and ribs of 170 burned planes. Caskets lined the parade field, pending burial of 2,403 civilians and military men. What upset Jack the most, however, were the pictures that couldn't be taken: hulls of the USS *Utah* and USS *Arizona* in their graves under the surface of the bay. In the holds of the two ships rested the bodies of 1,177 crew members.

Jack also read an interview of a Marine recruiter. He noted the address of the recruiting office in Dallas.

The next morning, Jack drove his car to Dallas. He dropped Tuttle and Yeager off at the train station. Then he went downtown and enlisted in the Marine Corps. He took his physical and drove back to Ennis to await the results.

A couple of weeks later, Jack stopped at the Ennis Post Office and picked up a letter addressed to him. The envelope had an official-looking postage-free frank on one corner and, on the other, the return address of the Dallas Marine Corps recruiting center.

Jack ripped the letter open. He scanned the short message. Then he ran home and leapt over the front porch railing. Waving the letter aloft, he hollered to his mother. "I've been accepted, I've been accepted," he shouted.

"I'm a Marine."

On Thursday, January 22, 1942, Jack returned to the Marine Corps' office at Dallas. A recruiter swore him into the Corps. Standing with the other enlistees, he repeated the oath:

> *I will bear true faith and allegiance to the United States of America. I will serve them honestly and faithfully against all their enemies whomsoever. And I will obey the orders of the President of the United States and the orders of the officers appointed over me, according to the Rules and Articles for the Government of the Army, Navy, and Marine Corps of the United States.*

A photographer from the *Dallas Morning News* snapped a shot of Jack, his right hand raised.

By the time the picture ran in the paper the next day, Jack had gone back home and packed his razor and a change of underwear in his bag. He parked his car at his parents' home, leaving strict instructions that someone in the family keep it polished until he came home again.

On Friday evening, Jack's sister, Thelma, filled the gas tank of her car. Her mother climbed in the back seat beside Aunt Nannie and Cousin Bertha. Jack sat next to Thelma. They drove the 50 miles to Dallas.

"Doesn't Jack look handsome?" Thelma asked, patting her brother's knee. "Oh, I'm so proud of him."

When they reached Dallas, Thelma drove to the train depot. Jack opened the door and hopped out.

"I'll say so long here. I don't want you to see me off," he insisted. He kissed each of them in turn, then hurried through the big double doors. He turned around and took one last look. Tears sprang to Thelma's eyes. Her heart felt like a lead balloon. She drove away from the train station, wondering if she would ever see her brother again.

In the back seat, Nannie noticed that Laura's face had turned ashen. Nannie put her arms around her sister and held her all the way back to Ennis. When they got home, Jack's mother went to bed. The doctor had recently diagnosed Laura's condition as heart trouble.

Aboard the troop train bound for San Diego, Jack found himself with a job to do. The sergeant took a look at the enlistees he was taking to boot camp and asked Jack to help him. Not only was Jack tall but he was also the only recruit aboard older than 21. Those two characteristics, the sergeant decided, gave Jack an air of authority. The sergeant figured Jack could handle just about any situation and put him in charge of watching out for the others.

Jack took his responsibility seriously. If he saw a skinny kid, he'd make sure the boy got plenty to eat. If he noticed a sad look on someone's face, he diagnosed it as homesickness. Jack would sit beside the boy, find him a cup of coffee, tell him a joke. Pretty soon the youngster would be laughing, or at least smiling.

On January 30, 1942, the Giants crossed Jack Lummus'

name off their roster. That same day, the train carrying Jack crossed the border into California. As he stepped off the train in San Diego, I was standing straight while Mother pinned the hem of my dress.

I didn't dream that anything in my future could be more exciting than wearing the red-and-white-striped dress to the senior prom.

CHAPTER SEVEN

MARCHING BOOTS

In January 1942, I trudged through knee-deep snow to school. At the end of the day, I joined my friends uptown. We met at the drugstore where we perched on stools like a line of sparrows on a fence.

Our conversations concerned bylines in the school paper or getting a passing grade in history or whether Junior Falk would ever ask one of us to jitterbug with him. We didn't bother with world events, such as Gen. Douglas MacArthur's retreat to the Bataan Peninsula. Our interests revolved around our team's standing in the state basketball tournament. We didn't think too much beyond the horizon we could see out there on the Great American Prairie.

When troop trains began to pass through town, however, our small world expanded a bit. My girlfriends and I would hurry down to the CB&Q depot and wave at boys looking out at us through steam-sweated windows. If the train stopped, a spunky girl might scribble her address on a scrap of notebook paper and pass it up to the cute G.I. standing on the iron steps.

The emotions of the boys on those trains and the girls they left at home swung wildly from excitement to depression. As the young fellow boarded the troop train, he and his sweetheart vowed everlasting love. As soon as he got settled, they would marry. The girl began her lonely vigil at the post office. Postmarks on the letters came from Army camps farther and farther away. The boy pestered his corporal. Where are we going? he asked. What'll my APO address be? Maybe she waited, and maybe she didn't.

The generals and admirals running the war assured mothers, wives, and sweethearts that their draftees would come home in a year. Those who studied recent events in Europe didn't believe it.

Separation weakened the supports of family, church, and custom just when a young person needed them the most. The lack of supports sapped one's ability to cope with a rapidly changing lifestyle. Gone forever was the day when a girl graduated from high school and worked a year or two at J. C. Penney's before she married the boy next door. That boy had boarded a Greyhound bus and gone off to National Guard camp at Fort

Robinson, Arkansas.

That happened in my hometown. Shortly after I graduated in May 1942, my classmates vanished overnight. The boys joined the Army or Air Corps or Navy. The girls left, too. They went to the Martin Bomber plant in Omaha to rivet B-17s or to the munitions plant in Grand Island to pour black powder into bombshells. Some moved to Washington, D. C., to work for civil service or to the West Coast where the boys were. Thousands of boys.

I couldn't decide what to do. Dad offered to send me to journalism school at Creighton University. After barely cracking a book in high school, however, I knew that four years in college would waste Dad's money and my time. So I gave up my part-time jobs and went to work as reporter for the *Holdrege Daily Citizen*. Mother had left my dad by then, so he and I took turns washing dishes for the next year.

Meanwhile, when Jack Lummus stepped off the train in San Diego, he saw a long line of trucks parked under shabby palm trees. He milled about the depot platform with the other recruits. He felt disoriented, unsure of what was expected of him. Officers stalked around like banty roosters, flaunting their authority. Noncommissioned officers, their flannel shirt sleeves busy with stripes, consulted rosters snapped onto clipboards.

"Answer up when your name is called," a corporal hollered. He waved the enlistees into beds of canvas-covered trucks.

The military "taxis" pulled away from the curb and rumbled in low gear through downtown San Diego. There, sailors wearing dark blue winter uniforms swaggered up and down the sidewalks. Their white hats bobbed like foam on the ocean's swells.

Pulling onto a highway, the trucks drove a short distance north. Just past Lindbergh Field and the rambling Ryan Aircraft plant, they turned onto a sand spit.

Jack saw a compound laid out like forts the Army built during the American Indian wars. Two-story barracks, connected by arched arcades, faced a graveled parade ground. The buildings looked like Spanish haciendas with their yellow stucco walls and red tile roofs.

But Jack quickly realized they were not stopping for lunch at a hospitable village. Military barrage balloons floated overhead, and the trucks rolled under a sign proclaiming: RECRUIT TRAINING DEPOT, MARINE CORPS BASE, SAN DIEGO, CALIF. This was Mainside, one of the Marine Corps' two training centers, which everyone called boot camps. Those who enlisted at recruiting centers east of the Mississippi River received their initial training at Parris Island, South Carolina. All others came here to Mainside.

They rode past "old salts," Marines about to graduate from two months of boot training. The veterans stopped what they were doing and jeered at the white-shirted recruits: "You'll be sor-ree!"

At an isolated corner of the base, they arrived at a row of tents pegged into sandy ground. Non-commissioned officers, or NCOs, greeted the newcomers and ordered them to form lines.

Some of the noncoms slapped swagger sticks against their thighs. They curled their lips as if disgusted by what the recruiter had sent them. All wore brimmed, hard-felt hats, reminding Jack of the Texas Rangers.

One of the drill instructors glared at the ragged line and muttered an obscenity. Another spit tobacco juice at a recruit's shoes. A sergeant called roll. His gravelly voice competed with commands barked at a platoon drilling on the parade grounds. Jack and the other boots, or trainees, stared in envy. Would they ever be that snappy? Would they learn to cut such sharp corners?

A sergeant marched Jack and the other nervous recruits to a warehouse-like building. The boots stripped off their clothes and stood patiently while doctors poked and prodded them and medics inoculated them with blunt hypodermic needles. Then they dressed and double-timed to a long building. Corporals shunted the green-horns into an auditorium where they spent the afternoon taking a battery of intelligence and aptitude tests.

A quartermaster handed out blankets and pillows. Jack held out his arms to receive a pith helmet, socks, overcoat, and a seabag to store them in. A surly sergeant threw a cot, pad, and half shelters, or one-man tents, at him. He was issued a pail and directed to the canteen. There a sergeant filled the pail with toothpaste and shaving cream and a scrub brush.

"Thank you, sir," Jack said. He'd already learned to

add "sir" when speaking to a superior officer.

"Don't thank me, boot," the sergeant growled. "You'll pay for all these goodies out of your first paycheck."

Back at their tents, they counted off and were divided into four platoons of 64 men each. A corporal took charge of Jack's platoon. He strutted around, glowering and swearing and shaking his head.

"I'll make Marines out of you yellow-livered sisters if it kills 75 percent of you in the bargain," he growled. "Just remember this, though. Until I do, you'll be called 'privates' or 'boots.' You won't be called Marines until you graduate and earn the privilege of wearing the world's proudest uniform." He marched the recruits over to the mess hall. After they ate, the corporal dismissed them.

Exhausted, Jack fell onto his cot and slept until 0450, or 10 minutes until five in the morning. He would have stayed abed later, but the bare bulb that dangled from the top of the tent flashed on, awakening him. Then the drill instructor shrilled his whistle, and Jack jumped out of bed.

"Okay, all you blockheads," the DI shouted, striding up and down the line of bunks, "on your feet." Jack lumbered into the "head," which he knew by then not to call a bathroom. He shaved and tugged on his dungarees and shuffled outside. He stood with the other recruits in a zigzag line, shivering in the damp, chilly dawn. The DI chastised them with a long succession of cusswords, all meaning incompetent. Then he double-timed them to the mess hall for scrambled eggs and hot coffee.

In the next few days, Jack began to see a pattern

evolve. First thing every morning, from Monday through Saturday, the platoon lined up for inspection. Then, after calisthenics, they spent the rest of the day executing drills and sitting in classrooms.

Jack memorized "The Marine's Handbook" and studied Marine Corps history. He sat through lectures on military courtesy and discipline and stood at attention, at ease, parade rest, about face. He learned to read a compass and maps and practiced scouting and patrolling.

He studied battle techniques, such as using ditches for protection against bullets. He learned to minimize casualties by not bunching up. It got easy for him to take catnaps while marching in column. And the platoon marched everywhere: to chow, to the pool, often on the double. They marched to see an Orson Welles movie at the theater and to the quartermaster's to draw more equipment.

Along with the rest of it, Jack learned to hate. The drill instructor aroused hatred of the enemy by telling stories about Japanese cruelties during their war with the Chinese. More than the Japanese, though, the recruits learned to hate their drill sergeant. He was a harsh taskmaster. Let one of them mess up, and the DI punished the entire platoon. "Double-time until church," he would bark, or "No church this week." For an unforgivable sin, he ordered the sinner to "high port around the parade grounds." That meant jogging with a heavy rifle held at shoulder height.

The DI knew that the training platoon hated him; he

brought it about on purpose. It was the first step in molding 64 individuals into a smooth, machinelike team. After boot camp, each platoon would contain only 40 men.

It worked with the boot from Ennis, Texas. Jack was no longer Jack Lummus. He was a serial number. By spending every waking moment with his unit, he lost his identity and became a cog in a wheel. His new life was a world away from his mother's fried chicken or the heft of a silky ash baseball bat.

The second step involved the most valuable lesson of all, a lesson that would save some of their lives one day. The platoon had learned to follow orders the instant they heard the command. Obedience without question linked the platoon into a cohesive unit that would hang together under stress of battle.

The guys hung around together in their spare time, too. The time Jack liked best was around nine in the evening, or 2100, when the hillbillies keened their "down home" songs or the guys gathered around the tripod-supported canvas lister bag that held their drinking water. They listened to someone whistling "Chattanooga Choo Choo" or someone else playing "Blues in the Night" on his harmonica. Then they shot the breeze and talked about women. They talked about the platoon, too, with pride in their voices. They were better than the others, weren't they? Cut corners like a knife, didn't they? Had the sharpest DI.

By the end of the second week, Jack had turned into an "old salt." Whenever a truck ground through camp with its cargo of raw boots, Jack hooted: "You'll be sor-ree."

They got cocky, figuring they had learned everything about being a Marine. Then the quartermaster dug Springfield M-1903 rifles out of the cases they'd been stored in since the First World War. The DI stood in the doorway of the tent, fieldstripping the rifle and reciting the names of its 100 parts. Fast as a whippet the sergeant replaced the tiny springs and screws. Then he double-timed the boots over to open-air cleaning stalls. Instructors passed around screw drivers and brushes and handed out buckets of sudsy water or cans of gasoline. The boots started scrubbing barrels and bayonets clean of the paraffin that had protected them from rust. By evening, the gummy grease smeared Jack from forehead to elbows. He stayed up all night repeatedly taking the vintage weapon apart, naming its pieces, and putting it back together. Before long, he could do the job blindfolded.

Every morning after chow the next week, the DI drilled the platoon with their rifles. "Side lunge, left side first. One, two, three, four. Up and out by the numbers. Up and on shoulders by the numbers."

If a boot dropped his firearm, the DI ordered him out on the parade ground. For three hours, he knelt and kissed his weapon, repeating, "I love my rifle, I love my rifle."

The training grew rougher. With his bayonet fixed, Jack lunged at straw-stuffed dummies that reminded him of the Giants' tackling dummies. He sprinted 100 yards, his vision hampered by a gas mask, his chest heaving from lack of oxygen.

Jack practiced tossing live hand grenades. Pull the pin. Throw the grenade. "You got five seconds before it explodes," the DI shouted. "One Mississippi, two Mississippi..." Hit the deck. Don't creep; roll out of the fall.

He practiced hand-to-hand combat with the short-bladed Kabar knives or snapped imaginary bullets at phantom enemy Zeroes. He crawled on his stomach 65 yards through sand and barbed wire, with live machine-gun bullets zinging overhead.

When the sunset gun sounded, the platoon marched back to the tent, exhausted and thirsty. Jack lay on his cot at night, too tired to sleep. He wondered why he'd been so eager to join the Marines. He regretted leaving the Giants. Even so, he felt himself growing tougher, getting prouder with every passing hour.

After a month at Mainside, the platoon piled into trucks again. Several miles north of San Diego, they got off at Camp C. B. Matthews. Expert marksmen taught them to shoot their rifles.

Jack twisted his long body into painful positions and aimed. He held his breath and practiced firing without bullets. He calculated elevation and adjusted his rear ladder sight for wind speed and direction. Then the corporal issued bullets.

"Ready on the right, ready on the left, ready on the firing line. Commence firing."

Jack filled the sheets of his score book, a record that

would follow him for the duration of his Marine career. He fired at targets 200, 300, and 500 yards away. He fired standing, kneeling, prone, sitting. He marked his score for slow, then rapid, fire. He'd heard that boots who didn't qualify would go to cooks and bakers school.

Finally, Jack and the other recruits returned to Mainside. They volunteered for combat training or took exams for specialist schools. They were evaluated and put through more physical fitness tests.

The quartermaster issued Jack a khaki colored flannel shirt and olive-green wool blouse and trousers. He pinned the Marine emblem on his overseas caps. Now the noncoms no longer called Jack a boot. He had earned the right to be addressed as "Mac."

Then he got paid and discovered the deductions. The shaving cream and toothpaste weren't free. The final blow struck when he learned that Marines, unlike soldiers and sailors, didn't get a week's furlough after boot camp. Instead, Jack would go to his next duty station: Company C at Camp Elliott, 10 miles north of San Diego.

In two months at boot camp, Jack had changed. He had absorbed what it meant to be a part of a military machine. No longer was he a football end or a center-fielder. He wasn't a Big Man on Campus or a police officer's son. No longer was he a boot or recruit, either. *Now* he was a Marine.

CHAPTER EIGHT

"PLAY BALL"

For the first four months after Pearl Harbor, the news coming out of the Pacific sent chills down the spines of Americans. War correspondents reported Japanese invasions of one strategic island after the other. Citizens along the West Coast feared their shores would be Japan's next target. Men and women, and even children, armed themselves with an odd assortment of weapons and patrolled the beaches.

Then the United States went on the offensive, and the picture changed. Americans took heart when they learned that the aircraft carrier, USS *Hornet*, had steamed to within 700 miles of Tokyo. A squadron of medium bomber planes led by Lt. Col. James Doolittle lifted off its decks. The pilots flew to Tokyo and dumped their bombs. Then they scurried another thousand miles to safety in China.

With a mixture of hope and uncertainty, Jack Lummus traveled a few miles north from Mainside to Camp Elliott. There he joined a line company, where he would be molded into a skilled fighter.

At Elliott's advanced weapons range, Jack fired more complicated artillery than the simple Springfield rifle he had trained on at Mainside. He also learned to take apart and reassemble a carbine, a Browning Automatic Rifle, known as the BAR, and the lightweight Thompson submachine gun.

During the work week, Jack dressed in dungarees. For Saturday morning inspections and parade drills, he changed into green wool trousers, khaki-colored flannel shirt, and field scarf. On his feet, he wore the clumsy serviceable boots called boondockers. Square on his head he wore a fore-and-aft overseas cap or a sun helmet. A pistol and canteen dangled from his waist. Whenever he wore his jacket, which Marines called a "blouse," the brown strap of a heavy, leather Sam Browne belt cut diagonally across his chest.

After inspection, the bugler blew "Who's going ashore?" Marines had waited all week for that signal. With six-hour passes in their pockets, they crammed into waiting buses. Soon the buses headed out the base gate, bound for San Diego. Liberty offered escape, a few hours of freedom from sergeants. Jack, however, spent more liberty hours on a baseball diamond than in San Diego. Nearly every West Coast military base sponsored football and baseball teams or boxing and wrestling matches. Base commanders took personal interest in scores—too personal, perhaps. Fitness reports and promotions often rode on a Marine's batting average or a coach's win-loss record.

Officers in charge of athletics or recreation scanned the personnel records of recruits transferring in from other bases or boot camp. They kept a sharp lookout for athletes. Capt. Harry Y. Maynard, the athletic director at Camp Elliott, was no exception.

In 1941, Captain Maynard organized the Devildogs, the San Diego Marine Corps baseball club. When a recruit with college or professional experience came to Elliott, the captain and his coach, Gunner W. R. Sonnenberg, brought him in to try out for the Devildogs.

Jack's baseball record with the Baylor Bears and the Wichita Falls Spudders caught their attention. After watching the lean Texan shag balls, they put him in at right field.

All the Devildogs except one, Cpl. M. L. Williams, were privates. Instead of the barracks, the team bunked in an athletic building. They were given the responsibility of taking care of Sergeant Duffy, Elliott's mascot. Duffy, a 110-pound English bulldog, was famous. It took a board five feet square to display his blue ribbons and trophies. He had sired all the English bulldog puppies that became mascots at other Marine Corps bases. Sergeant Duffy, who led all of Elliott's major parades, was busted to private once. During a parade, he lifted his leg and sprinkled a flag pole. The incident occurred in front of a reviewing stand full of dignitaries.

Except for having a dog, living with a group of fellows reminded Jack of life in a Baylor dormitory. As a student, he was always strapped for money. And he wasn't that much better off in the Marine Corps. At that time, Marine privates earned only $21 a month. Jack and his teammates conserved their money by sharing.

"Any night we could afford it, we'd pool our coins and send out for baloney, bread, chips, and pop," said Cy Williams, the Devildog's centerfielder.

When payday rolled around once a month, the team-mates might splurge and ride the bus into San Diego for a while. The rest of the time, they worked out at the base.

The team as a whole carried a .347 batting average. Their top batter was Hal Hirshon, a former University of California at Los Angeles athlete who, like Jack Lummus, had starred in both baseball and football. Hirshon led the Devildogs in homeruns and wound up the season with a .439 batting average.

The Devildogs made a name for themselves playing the schedule Captain Maynard lined up. They lost only two of the 74 games against teams at other West Coast military bases. With that record, Maynard proposed taking the Devildogs on the road with a snappy drill team. He figured the excitement of the game and the romance of the marching team would attract enlistments.

Maynard's suggestion, however, didn't get to first base. With the war in the Pacific heating up, Maynard's superior officers couldn't allow such foolishness. In May 1942,

Sgt. Duffy, mascot of the U.S. Marine Corps training base at San Diego, lived in the barracks with Jack Lummus. Jack and other members of the Devildogs baseball team housed and cared for the famous English bulldog. Sgt. Duffy achieved fame during the 1940s as the sire of mascots at many Marine Corps bases. Duffy had so many blue ribons that it took a board five-feet by five-feet to display them. Duffy, who led all major parades at the base, was once demoted to private for urinating on a flag pole in front of dignitaries on the reveiwing stand. (Courtesy Cy Williams)

they broke up the Devildogs and transferred its players elsewhere.

The Marine Corps had decided to make military policemen out of its taller men. Jack's six-foot-four frame drew their attention, and in May 1942, they transferred him into a guard company at Mare Island.

Mare Island, a peninsula rather than an island, was located about 50 miles north of San Francisco. With its huge shipyards, long docks, and mammoth cranes, it was one of the California coast's busiest military installations.

Jack stood at one of the shipyard's gates. He checked identifications of thousands of men and women who worked three shifts a day, seven days a week. Those workers took great pride in the part they played in aiding the war effort. They built some of the 10,000-ton Liberty ships launched by West Coast shipbuilders at the rate of two a day.

But Jack found guard duty dull and boring. When he joined the Marine Corps, he had hoped to be shipped right out to a Pacific battle zone. He had expected to be living in a tent on a sun-drenched island; instead, his quarters were in a cold, concrete barracks. He thought he would be slashing his way through the jungle with a machete; instead, he slogged two miles every morning through a bone-chilling fog to drink coffee at the mess hall.

As Jack had always done ever since he could hold a bat, he found a baseball game. A Marine colonel at Mare Island had organized another ball club. The roster included Jack Casey and several other members from the

When Jack Lummus (the tallest man on the back row) was transferred to Mare Island Naval Station in northern California, he joined the Marine Corps baseball team. (Courtesy Cy Williams)

Devildogs. So Jack put on another striped gray uniform and joined the team.

One of the team's outfielders was 20-year-old Hank Bauer, a minor league player destined for post-war fame with the New York Yankees. Bauer showed such talent that the colonel finagled to get his name removed whenever it turned up on the overseas assignment lists.

"Can't lose my outfielder," he'd say. "Best team I've ever had."

Then a United States senator began to criticize professional athletes who played baseball or football rather than join units overseas. He singled out Hank Bauer as one of the athletes on easy duty. "Cush duty," the senator called it. Despite the colonel's efforts to keep him, Bauer volunteered to join the Marine Raiders.

A short time afterward, Jack received a promotion. On June 10, 1942, he made private first class. Two months later, he was promoted to corporal.

All that summer and into the fall of 1942, news from the Pacific seesawed between good and bad. The United States Navy crushed the Japanese fleet at the Battle of Midway. Then Japanese troops occupied two of the Aleutian Islands, uncomfortably close to Alaska. On August 7, the First Marine Division landed on Guadalcanal. The enemy's navy forced American ships to withdraw, leaving the Marines stranded. For the next six months, the First Marines fought not only a zealous enemy but also fatigue, disease, and dwindling food and ammunition. Finally the United States Navy outwitted the Japanese fleet and came to the troops' rescue. The Marines finally secured the strategic island in February 1943.

Back in America, those ominous dispatches stunned us. No longer could we believe that the war would end in one year. That timetable became even less trustworthy when the government decided to ration commodities. Congressmen decreed that "our boys in uniform" needed cheese and shoes more than we in the States needed ice cream and tires. For the first time in my life, I tore red and blue coupons out of a ration book. I stood in line to buy a pound of coffee, hoping to get the Chase and Sanborn brand. More often I came home with an odd brand made bitter with the addition of chicory.

Then meat went on the rationed list. I found recipes in

Good Housekeeping guaranteed to make Dad eat canned Spam and swear it was roast pork. Butter took coupons, too, but you could buy all the margarine you wanted. The Food and Drug Administration, spurred on by the dairy farmers, issued a ruling that prohibited the sale of yellow margarine. In each carton of margarine, you found a packet of reddish-orange coloring. My least favorite chore was to blend the food coloring into that lard-like, white spread.

The military needed metal, so it took more of my coupons for canned fruit and vegetables. Silk went into parachutes, and silk stockings disappeared from the shelves. We wouldn't see nylons for at least another year. When it was cold, I wore bulky, unbecoming cotton hose. I detested those lisle hose because they sagged in wrinkles around my ankles. More often, I shaved my legs and went bare-legged. When leg make-up came on the market, I tried that, too.

Dad had a coal furnace, so he didn't spend fuel oil coupons to heat the house. He walked to work and never used his allotted three gallons of gasoline a week. Some of his neighbors, however, put their cars up on blocks for the duration.

Just as the need for war materiel called for rationing, the demand for large numbers of tank drivers, fighter pilots, and torpedomen called for enlistments. American boys were being sent to fight on two bitterly contested fronts—either the South Pacific or North Africa. Such severe personnel shortages existed that in late 1942 the

Selective Service System lowered the draft age to 18. Millions of American boys between the ages of 19 and 21 swarmed into recruitment centers. They joined other services before the Army drafted them.

With all these enlistments, the Marine Corps started to expand. In the next three years, the Corps' four divisions would become six. Officers were needed to command those new platoons and companies and battalions that must be formed. The Corps decided that it had more important jobs for men like Jack Lummus than guarding the Mare Island shipyards.

Officials at Mare Island scouted around the base among their noncommissioned officers. They examined records. They looked for men with presence, personality, and good looks. They sought outstanding intellectual qualities and signs of leadership; they searched for loyalty and good judgment, integrity and reliability. More than any other criteria, they looked for men with guts.

They combed through Jack Lummus' record. A centerfielder who stretched the extra inches to make an impossible catch. A batter who planted his feet square at home plate and smashed the ball over the fence. A man who stole bases and slid to safety on bare skin. Those qualities added up to what they were looking for.

In October, the Marines enrolled Jack in officer candidate school. They cut his orders for the train ride to Quantico, Virginia.

CHAPTER NINE

GOLD BARS

Jack Lummus got up from the hard coach seat and walked toward the water fountain at the front of the railroad car. He stepped around servicemen who stood in the aisle or sprawled on the dirty floor, playing cards.

He filled a paper cup and shoved open the heavy door. Out in the vestibule between cars, piles of suitcases and seabags took up most of the floor space.

Bending, Jack stared through the soot-smeared window. The train ahead rounded a curve, and he caught sight of the engine. The engineer had hooked on two extra locomotives to haul the long line of cars up the Sierra Nevada Mountains. They were past Reno, headed now for the Rockies. He looked out at land so beautiful it made his throat ache. Maybe after the war, he would come back and walk through those pines.

First, though, he had to get through officer candidate

school. He strolled back to his seat, vowing to work hard and become a topnotch officer.

That night the train stopped at Salt Lake City. A woman with two small children got on, and Jack gave her his seat. He guessed she was on her way back East to spend a few days with her husband before he shipped out for England or the North African desert. Or she might be headed home to wait until her husband returned from the war.

Jack struggled through the crowded cars to the diner. He ordered coffee, which the porter brought in a heavy silver pot. Jack poured a cupful and raised it to his image in the night-blackened window. Happy 27th birthday, he told himself.

A couple of days later, the train pulled into Chicago. Jack got off and walked around, thinking about the day he had come through that station 10 months earlier. He felt a twinge, remembering the drubbing the Bears had given the Giants. He got back on the train.

The stop at Chicago started Jack on a trip down memory lane. He found himself reliving first downs and touchdowns as the train stopped at Pittsburgh and Philadelphia and then glided into New York City where he changed trains. When the train left Washington, D.C.'s Union Station, it rolled past Griffith Stadium. Jack felt his chest swell with pride. Right over there he had helped the Giants clinch the 1941 Eastern Division crown.

The train crossed into Virginia and headed for Quantico. Jack saw red-clay fields, ragged stands of a tobacco crop, and winter-brown oak trees. They reminded him of the Texas farmland he had grown up on.

A few short miles later, the train stopped at Quantico's small depot. Stiff-legged, Jack and the other OCS trainees stepped off. A sergeant loaded them into trucks, and they rode through the main gate to the administration building. The quartermaster issued them uniforms. They were bare of insignia except for the small, brass "OC" pinned to their shirt collars. Jack changed clothes and sat for a photograph.

Wandering around the base, Jack ran into two of his buddies from the Devildogs. Jack Casey had started OCS two weeks earlier, and Hal Hirshon would enter the same class as Jack.

Quantico's open, attractive grounds were different from Jack's other duty stations. His home for the next two months would be a big, red-brick barracks. It was far more comfortable than Mare Island's cement-block buildings and much warmer than the tents at San Diego.

Although the grounds were different, Jack found the schedule about the same. At 0555 every morning, a non-com blew a shrill police whistle. Jack got up and made his bed, regulation-style: tight so that a dime bounced on the top blanket. By 0630, he had showered, shaved, and dressed. He marched to the mess hall for eggs and bacon. After breakfast, he double-timed to the drill field and polished his quickstep.

Some of the instructors were noncommissioned officers. Most treated Jack and the other candidates with a lot more respect than the drill instructors had at boot camp. A couple even addressed them as "sir." A few, though, ridiculed and even punished the students by handing out bad "chits." A candidate might earn a bad chit for wearing his field scarf tucked into his shirt. "That's the way an Army dogface wears his scarf," an instructor would snarl. "I can arrange it if you'd rather be in the Army than the Marines."

The candidate who slipped up might find himself called in for "office hours," meaning that after the long day ended he would sit in an office filing or typing. Or he might be denied a privilege: a weekend pass, for example, or permission to make a telephone call or attend church or Mass.

Jack figured that the noncoms wanted to get in a few last-minute licks before their charges outranked them.

However, many instructors were officers, their blouses weighted down with lines of medals and decorations. These men treated the candidates like gentlemen. They employed wit and intelligence to teach mapping and safety, military history, etiquette, and hygiene.

The advanced courses in amphibious warfare taught Jack the Corps' special function: to invade an enemy's realm and prepare the way for engineers, the Army's infantry, and the military's construction battalion, called Seabees.

Jack became familiar with the newest weapons and acquired techniques and tactics that never left him. He learned to defend a platoon's perimeters, to protect its flanks, and to counter unexpected mortar fire. He studied ways to concentrate his forces on the enemy's weakest points, to align his troops effectively, and to press when he had the advantage. He devised advance plans and reviewed the age-old element of surprise.

Jack's instructors set up simulated battle situations, testing his ability to make snap decisions and act under stress. Had he failed to react promptly and correctly, he would have flunked. An officer who made a wrong decision during the heat of a battle cost lives—his life and the lives of men who relied upon him. Jack's 20 years in baseball and football stood him in good stead. When he caught a ball, whether in centerfield or at end, he had a split second to decide what to do. Should he throw the ball? Should he run with it? Slow, improper decisions lost ball games; hesitant, incorrect decisions lost battles. Jack passed the test successfully.

During his stint at Quantico, Jack seemed to step onto a new plateau of growth. Ever since he was a small boy, he had demonstrated his commitment to his family's welfare. When he played football or baseball, no one ever questioned his loyalty to his team. But now Jack was no longer a boy playing games in the sandlot behind the church. Whether he had consciously decided or not, Jack obligated himself to greater responsibilities. He accepted the responsibility for the lives of men he would lead into battle. He accepted the responsibility that came with maturity.

Jack developed a style of leadership that would earn

him the confidence and regard of those who served under him. He envisioned himself as a teacher and his men as students. He vowed never to scold a man in public and always to treat a man as an equal, not an inferior. He would expect a man to give the best that was in him to give; he would never ask a man to do anything that he himself couldn't do as well or better. If an underling deserved a promotion, Jack would recommend him. If Jack had to be tough, he would be tough as whale leather. But above all, he would always be fair.

Jack took responsibility for his appearance, too. In his spare time, he laundered, starched, and ironed his fatigues, spit-shined his shoes, and cleaned his uniform with carbon tetrachloride. If he felt rich on a corporal's pay of $42 a month, he went on a weekend pass to Washington, D.C. He found it easy to strike up a conversation with a girl. During wartime, there were six girls to every man in the nation's capitol. On other weekends, he toured George Washington's home, Mount Vernon. Or he joined the swarms of Marines, soldiers, and sailors on the boardwalk at Colonial Beach, competing for a girl's smile. He ate seafood at a crab shed where newspapers served as tablecloths. More often, though, Jack stayed at Quantico and lined up impromptu softball or touch football games on the sports field.

After six weeks at Quantico, graduation rolled around. Jack Casey graduated on December 16. Two weeks later, Jack Lummus got measured for a green wool second lieutenant's uniform. He cleaned the bore of his M-1 rifle with the steam hose. He pressed razor-sharp pleats down the trouser legs of his new uniform.

On December 30, 1942, a Wednesday, Jack stood for a final, rigorous rifle inspection. Then Lt. Gen. Thomas A. Holcomb, commandant of the entire Marine Corps, stepped to the podium and addressed the graduates. The general spoke of courage and loyalty, tradition and ritual. When the graduates pinned gold bars on their uniforms, they deserved to feel proud, he said. They would go out to lead platoons and companies, strengthened by the qualities of leadership they had learned at Quantico.

"Leadership is not easy," he said. "It is not automatic. You must possess those qualities that command respect and loyalty. You must inspire the determination and compelling desire to work together for a common end. No graph, no chart, no rules and regulations or other printed words can take the place of such leadership. May you have it to the greatest degree possible."

Jack Lummus stood then, straighter and taller than before, to receive his gold bars. Inside him remained vestiges of the bright-eyed boy from a Texas cotton farm. But now, after six sweat-tough weeks of teaching him and testing him, the Corps awarded Jack a second lieutenant's commission. This certified him as an officer—and a gentleman. Those who knew Jack never doubted the latter.

Immediately after the ceremony, Jack left Quantico. He boarded the train at the shabby depot. Changing trains in Washington and again in New York, he headed across country for San Diego. In his pocket were his lieutenant's pay of $125 and his orders to return to Camp Elliott. He would assume his first duties as a Marine officer.

A couple of days later, the Union Pacific train with Jack aboard stopped a few minutes at Kearney, Nebraska. Jack stepped off and walked up and down the platform, his heels crunching against the snow-covered bricks. Twenty-five miles south, at Holdrege, I sat in the Sun Theater, engrossed in *Holiday Inn*, Bing Crosby's latest movie. After the show, I walked over to Nelson's Confectionery for a chocolate coke. I inserted a nickel in the juke box and punched the 78-speed recording of the movie's hit song: "I'm Dreaming of a White Christmas."

Never in my wildest dreams did I imagine that the next New Year's Eve I would be in California, dancing with a tall, gentlemanly, fun-loving, handsome Texan named Jack Lummus.

CHAPTER TEN

ROADS TO CALIFORNIA

Jack Lummus arrived at Camp Elliott and hurried to the administration building to pick up his orders as advanced combat training officer. Dozens of times, his hand flew to his forehead in a salute as he met enlisted men along the way. Eight months earlier, *he* had been the lowly private making certain he saluted every officer who crossed his path. The tables had turned.

Now he would be the second lieutenant who smelled of Old Spice and looked as if he knew the score. Now, too, it would be Jack's responsibility to teach a group of greenhorns how to survive. He would have to prepare them to endure suffocating jungles of islands they'd never heard of, to outwit vicious opponents they'd never met.

Jack started his charges off with a tough regimen of

calisthenics. Skinny teenagers performed endless sit-ups. Flabby 20-year-olds ran obstacle courses. Four abreast, they crawled up and down landing nets as if abandoning ship. If they didn't know how to swim, they at least learned to float. They piled out of amphibious vessels and crawled ashore under an umbrella of blank bullets from machine guns and artillery weapons.

Instructors trained Jack's troops in judo and jujitsu, two ancient Japanese fighting methods. Farm boys learned to surprise an opponent. Disarm him, they were told. Break his hold, trip him, drop onto his chest. Shove your knees into his ribs. Finish him off. Be quick about it. Don't make a sound.

They called it survival.

Charles Doolittle, a Michigan schoolteacher, spent seven or eight weeks learning survival tactics from Jack. "We admired Lieutenant Lummus. Even behind his back, we willingly called him 'mister' or 'lieutenant.'"

Doolittle also admired the kindness with which Jack treated the men under him. "I saw Jack in the mess hall one day, talking to a boy who looked blue and homesick. He put an arm around the kid's shoulders and told him to go get a second helping." The boy walked away with a smile on his face.

The Michigan private became better acquainted with Jack when they both signed up to play baseball in May 1943. This wasn't the Devildogs of the year before. Gone was coach Harry Maynard, replaced by Lt. Dutch Broshelle. Gone were centerfielder Cy Williams and heavy hitter Hal Hirshon. Back was Jack Casey. Casey and Broshelle, like Jack Lummus, had just graduated from Quantico. Broshelle put Casey in at third base and Jack Lummus at centerfield. Private Doolittle played left field.

Outfitted in gray uniforms with "U.S. Marine Corps" stenciled across the shirts, the ball club started playing scheduled games against other service teams from the San Diego vicinity. "We played Saturday and Sunday afternoons, and evenings, too, if there was a lighted field," recalled Doolittle. The teams didn't make up a regular league, Doolittle explained. "Watching the games just gave the men something to do."

The games were lively and rather informal, Doolittle said. At one game, Jack Lummus prevented a brawl. The players started grumbling about the umpire's "inexact calls." Before Jack's team went up to bat the next time, Jack walked over and conferred with the opponent's coach. They agreed to send the umpire home and let Jack take his place. Jack's fair and honest calls solved the problem, Doolittle said. "He didn't put up with any arguments, either."

Doolittle and Casey left the team in mid-June when the Marine Corps shipped them to Australia. Dutch Broshelle and Jack Lummus escorted Jean Casey down to the docks to see her husband off. A year later, Jack Casey died on Saipan.

Meanwhile, Marine Corps officials decided they had made a mistake the year before when they broke up the Devildogs and the Mare Island baseball teams. Such

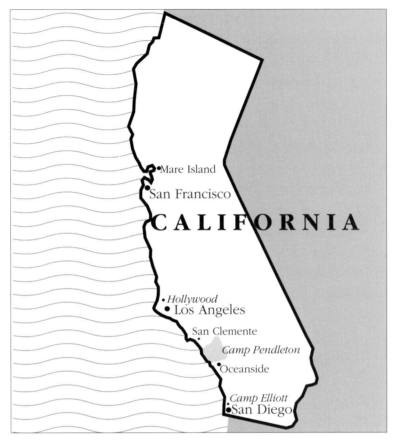

games had entertained thousands of bored youth stationed on the West Coast. Those boys had been uprooted
from their hometowns and shipped hundreds of miles
away from schoolrooms and jobs, from families and
friends. They became unruly. Worse, they started going
AWOL—going back home without being granted leave.

Then the Marine Corps discovered the wealth of professional athletes and All-American football stars stationed

at California bases. Commandants decided to tap that talent by expanding their athletic programs. They called them physical education, or combat conditioning. By the time Jack came back from the East, almost every military base on the West Coast sponsored either a baseball or a football team. Sometimes both.

The Corps brought Gene Tunney, a world champion boxer, to Camp Elliott. Tunney, a Hall of Famer, brought other well-known boxers with him to train boys from bases around San Diego.

Tunney sat in the bleachers one day and watched Jack Lummus knock in a winning run. Tunney talked Jack into working out with the boxers. But when Tunney tried to persuade him to join his staff as a trainer, Jack turned him down. "No, thanks," he responded. "I joined the Marines to fight the Japanese. And that's what I'd better do."

Jack volunteered for combat duty. "Don't worry, I'll be okay," he wrote his sister, Thelma.

The Marine Corps didn't ship Jack thousands of miles into the Pacific then. Instead, in June 1943, they transferred him 60 miles north to Oceanside, where a huge new camp was being built.

Three months later, in September 1943, I stepped off the Southern Pacific train at Pasadena, California. Jeanne and Barbara Bader, daughters of the Methodist minister, had helped me decide what to do. They invited me to move to California with them.

We rented a tiny house in Glendale and started hunting

jobs. I went to work as a secretary for one of the big defense plants. It turned into a humiliating experience, for I didn't fit in. My business wardrobe consisted of a navy blue suit, ordered out of a Montgomery Ward catalog. Even my high school typing skills left something to be desired. So when the woman I had replaced wanted to come back, the company let me go. I was stunned; that was the first and only time in my life I had lost a job.

My roommates and I pooled our savings and managed to pay the second month's rent. For a week, though, we lived on saltines and milk. Then we all went to work in a small factory down the street. There we waterproofed large cylinders that would hold supplies parachuted to ground troops.

More benefits than a paycheck resulted from that job, however. One of my co-workers, student of a Hollywood voice coach, arranged an audition for me. Annabelle Reinberg accepted me as a student. For the next two years, I rode the bus every week to her Laurel Canyon studio for lessons.

Then everything happened at once. Barbara married a Marine and moved to a base on the California desert. Jeanne moved in with a college friend. I met a young woman from Omaha, Lois Gerdes. Lois had leased an 18-room mansion on Los Feliz Boulevard in North Hollywood. To finance $100-a-month rent, she needed me and four other roommates to move in.

Out of the blue, my mother arrived in Los Angeles. She informed me that the break with my father could never be mended. Another man had entered her life. She took over the maid's quarters and assumed the role of housemother.

Mother and I both went to work at Occidental Life Insurance Company's home office at Sixth and Main streets in downtown Los Angeles. To get to work, we rode the red streetcar an hour morning and evening.

Then on December 17, 1943, a Friday night, I happened to be walking along Sunset Boulevard with Kay Cusamano, one of my roommates. Kay and I had been dancing at the Palladium that evening and were headed for the bus that would take us home. We strolled along, looking at the Christmas displays in the window of a Hollywood department store.

Coming up the street toward us were two Marine officers. One short and squat, one ever so tall and slim.

CHAPTER ELEVEN

GREENHORNS AND RAIDERS

In 1942, the federal government bought 180 square miles of California land halfway between San Diego and Los Angeles. Soon, workmen swarmed over the grounds, remodeling the Old Santa Margarita Ranch into a new Marine Corps base. Crews built mess halls and base hospitals. They put up rectangular structures to serve as post exchanges, chapels, and company headquarters. They installed a theater and set up Quonset huts for administrative offices. Everywhere among those buildings and around the perimeter sat the tents that would house hordes of Marines. They would arrive soon.

The Corps named the base for Maj. Gen. Joseph H. Pendleton, father of Marine Corps activities on the West Coast. Camp Pendleton would be the largest, both in size and population, of all Marine training centers.

Atomic bomb experiments taking place at Los Alamos,

New Mexico, and Oak Ridge, Tennessee, were among America's best-kept wartime secrets. Another was the November 1945 deadline to invade the Japanese mainland. But the best-kept secret of all was the estimate of casualties that invasion would cost. The commanders in charge of the assault figured that at least one million American men and boys would be either killed or wounded before the Japanese surrendered.

To prepare for such a huge invasion, the admirals and generals in Washington decided to add another Marine division to the four that already existed. They would need 22,500 men to staff and service the Fifth Division. There would be infantrymen and riflemen and flame throwers and artillerymen. To support those men, there would be cooks and medics and tank drivers and reconnaissance pilots. Enlistment centers scoured the countryside for recruits. Those who passed the physicals were rushed to boot camps at Parris Island and San Diego. Thousands of greenhorns were on their way to Camp Pendleton.

Lieutenants and captains were lined up to lead the squads, platoons, and companies that would be formed. Majors and colonels were promoted to command the battalions and regiments needed to operate the division.

Col. Ray A. Robinson, director of training at the new base, started a manhunt. He requisitioned Quantico's brightest graduates. He scoured records at Camp Lejeune, Parris Island, and Camp Elliott, looking for their most outstanding instructors. In June of 1943, he chose Jack Lummus.

Jack arrived at Camp Pendleton and found himself attached to the new Twenty-seventh Regiment. He pinned on silver first lieutenant's bars and got busy making room for the troops that started to trickle in.

The trickle turned into a deluge. Trainloads carrying recruits chugged down from Los Angeles to Oceanside. Railroad coach cars full of kids fresh from boot camp arrived in San Diego. Buses shuttled them up north to Camp Pendleton. With them came graduates from advanced training centers at Camp Elliott and Lejeune. Guadalcanal veterans, their wounds sewn up, wandered in from the military hospitals.

Then in January 1944, the Marine Corps decided to disband the battalions known as Raiders and Paratroopers. Those battalions were pulled off the Solomon Islands and boarded troopships headed for San Diego. When the ships dropped anchor, these seasoned fighters climbed into trucks and rode up Highway 101 to Camp Pendleton. The Paratroopers went into the Fifth Division's new Twenty-eighth Regiment. The battle-weary Second Raider Battalion was reassigned to the Twenty-seventh. About 100 Raiders joined the Third Battalion's Company G.

Company G's temporary commander was First Lt. Jack Lummus.

Pvt. William Eslinger of Bismarck, North Dakota, met Jack when he, too, joined Company G. For the next 18 months, he often worked closely with Jack.

Company G was bivouacked in a rustic tent area that ringed the main camp. Eslinger slept on a cot; he bathed and shaved in icy groundwater that he trapped by damming up runoff.

Shortly after the Raiders arrived, Jack's temporary command was changed to Company F of the Second Battalion. Although the company moved into Camp Pendleton proper, they still lived in tents.

Jack's job would be a challenge. He would have to mold a mismatched group into a unified fighting unit. Half of his company were 18-year-old kids, in for the duration. They didn't think about much other than mail call and letters from the girls back home. The other half—the Raiders—were older, tougher, rougher, professional Marines. These proud commandos were hard-bitten fighters, well versed in jungle warfare. They had learned unique skills.

It quickly became apparent that Jack's skills as a company commander would be unique, as well.

For one thing, when Fox Company went out on the detested overnight maneuvers, Jack didn't stay back at his headquarters, dry and warm and comfortable. No, he went with them. He slept alongside his men, on the ground with snakes and bugs, and, frequently, skunks. He arose when reveille blew at 0400. In the dark hours before dawn, he drank the same bitter coffee and ate the same breakfast of half a hot dog, half an orange, half a bowl of oatmeal without milk. He also stepped around the rattlesnakes that slid out on the rocks to warm themselves. He endured the same hot weather that put 32 men in sickbay with mild sunstroke.

That alone earned their respect.

He even dressed in dungarees as his men did. And he wore his trademark: his old baseball cap turned sideways on his head. He carried a long corncob pipe that he never seemed to light. Sometimes he clenched it in his teeth, upside down. The men liked that about him, too.

The men grumbled, though, when Jack took them on stiff tactical marches. Always the athlete, Jack insisted that they build up their physical endurance. They hiked 26, sometimes 50, miles through mountains and over ridges. Often they covered terrain so steep that it was as difficult to march down into canyons as uphill out of them.

"To go on a hike with him, to march behind him, was to take two fast steps to his one," said Don Hamilton, a private from Indiana.

Word got around about the nickname given Jack by baseball fans at Wichita Falls, Texas. His men started to call him "Cactus Jack."

No one from Fox Company ever forgot the non-stop, 20-mile hike Jack took them on. "He said we would break the time record," recalled one of the participants, John Whipple.

Out to the boondocks they went. Everyone wore full, 75-pound packs and carried weapons. Officers didn't ordinarily burden themselves with as much weight as their troops. To Whipple's amazement, Jack did.

"His arms consisted of a light carbine, while we all carried at least a 10-pound M-1 rifle," Whipple said. But Jack carried a full pack, too. The lighter weapon was his only advantage.

As usual, Jack often backtracked to the end of the line. He cheered the marchers on and boosted their spirits. Then he jogged to the front again.

During a five-minute break, the men collapsed on their backs. Jack walked around, checking them, and passing around a bottle of water.

Everybody went the full 20 miles, all but a half dozen who got blisters and had to drop out. The other 200 Fox Company members completed the march in just under three hours. That broke the Camp Pendleton record.

"Boy, did that hike separate the men from the boys," exclaimed Harold Reynolds, a former Raider and one of the hikers. "That march will always come up at any Raider gathering. And not one of us would have had it any other way."

Nor would anyone in Company F have wanted to change things when they came in from the boondocks, cleaned up, and stood for weekly inspection.

Peter Rondero vividly remembers Jack inspecting Company F. "There he stood in khaki uniform, a giant of a man. Tough. The cap down to his forehead, his sharp darting eyes. He would come forward and bark, 'Company prepare for inspection.'" The order would come down to Rondero's platoon leader, Lt. Richard Tilghman. Then Jack, with Tilghman close behind, passed down the rows. He examined a Marine's M-1 rifle and looked over his uniform. He noted his military bearing. Occasionally, Jack stopped to ask a man his name and rank. If he detected a spot on a collar, a fleck of dust on a shoe, hair a fraction of an inch too long, he handed out demerits.

After inspection, came Saturday review. The 60-piece band lined up on the field. Drums rattled, trumpets blared, tubas growled. *"From the halls of Montezuma, to the shores of Tripoli."* The colors snapped in the breeze— the Stars and Stripes on one flagstaff, the Marine Corps' scarlet and gold flag on the other. The Fifth Division's nickname, "The Spearhead," inspired its emblem: a scarlet shield with a gold Roman numeral V pierced by a blue spearhead.

Rondero always got a lump in his throat when he paraded behind Jack with the rest of Fox Company. Jack looked like a poster-perfect Marine in his green wool uniform or suntans. Spit-polished and knife-pleated, he led Company F onto the parade grounds. He held his head high and proud like a man in charge, a man at peace with himself. Twelve abreast, the columns followed Jack. They synchronized their steps, tucked their chins. Their shoulders, their mouths, and their rifles—all squared. They stepped high. Marched, wheeled, and counter-marched.

Fox Company passed the review stand. A bugle call. "Eyes right," Jack barked. He saluted the dignitaries. A second later, the guidon bearer dipped the division flag and 200 heads snapped right.

Jack typified the ideal Marine, said Ted Johnson, "The kind you read about in adventure stories."

John Whipple agreed. Jack was a standout individual, "an incredible guy." Jack was his idol, Whipple admitted. "There was no finer Marine, no finer man."

Jack didn't win that kind of admiration by being everyone's buddy. Sure, he laughed and joked with his men. He revealed his wry sense of humor and displayed a softspoken, unassuming, easygoing manner. He saw good in everyone and neither yelled nor swore at the men.

But Jack was a tough taskmaster. Firm but fair. No matter what he ordered them to do, they soon discovered that he could do the same as well or better.

The style of training that Jack put the men through toughened and hardened them. It also toughened and hardened their determination to prove they couldn't be broken.

Eslinger called Jack "stern." He drilled into his men that they must not take the rigid training lightly. He warned them that war was brutal, that in combat it would be *them* or the enemy.

"He showed us what we had to do for ourselves," said Don Hamilton.

"I give Jack Lummus a great deal of credit for my own life," claimed John Whipple. "He taught us survival, and a lot of us did survive because of him."

Jack had kept the promises he had made to himself at Quantico.

CHAPTER TWELVE

FALLING IN LOVE

The two Marines walking toward Kay Cusamano and me on that unforgettable evening of December 17, 1943, reminded me of Mutt and Jeff, a couple of cartoon characters. One stood well above six feet. The other was shaped like Mister Five-by-Five: five feet tall, five feet around the middle. Encouraged by my roommate's flashing black Italian eyes, the short, squat one said, "Hello."

I kept walking, but Kay, a big city girl from Chicago, said, "Hi." In today's world, only a daredevil would stop and talk to a stranger. But 1943 belonged to a simpler time, a time when people trusted one another. So the four of us stopped. The tall Marine and I stood to one side. Kay and the other man, who I now saw wore captain's bars, were both gabby. They covered the ground strangers usually do when they meet. Where are you from? they both asked. Where do you work? he asked. Where are you stationed? she asked.

Orville Tuttle was recreation officer at El Toro Marine Air Base at Santa Ana. His friend, Jack Lummus, was a first lieutenant at Camp Pendleton. Before joining the Marines, they played football together for the New York Giants.

While Kay and Tuttle bantered, Jack and I said a few words to each other. I forgot what we said a long time ago. But I will never forget his gentle, courteous manner nor the glint of humor in his eyes.

We walked up the block to an all-night diner for a cup of coffee.

I remember strolling beside Jack and glancing up at him. He was so tall! I had recently dated an air cadet who was two inches shorter than I. My high heels added a couple of inches to my five feet seven inches. It had embarrassed me to dance with him. I had promised myself never to go out with anyone who wasn't at least six feet three. The man beside me, I would soon learn, was six-four.

Observing the lieutenant in the glare of the coffee shop's bright overhead lights, I decided that he looked mature and manly. Then I learned that he had attended two colleges and had played professional football and semiprofessional baseball. He had even lived in New York City once and knew his way around Manhattan Island. He didn't act like a "slicker," though. He had a down-home earthiness to him that reminded me of my big brother.

He looked rough-hewn compared to the fine-boned, blond-haired Swedish boys I grew up with. His high cheekbones and strong jaw gave him a rugged look that added to his air of maturity. It didn't surprise me when I later learned he was one-quarter Chickasaw. In the dimness of the street outside, I had looked at him and thought, *Gosh but he's homely!* Then he smiled at me, a warm and generous and teasing smile. A smile that softened his features and made his gray-green eyes sparkle. I took back the word "homely."

Before Kay and I stepped aboard our bus, Jack had my phone number.

He called the next afternoon and invited me to dinner.

When Jack rode up in a taxi, I asked him to dismiss it and come in to pass muster with my mother, whom I had begun calling Nancy. The two of them hit it off instantly. They sat in the living room, talking politics and football. I tapped my foot, impatient to be off on my date with the tall lieutenant from Ennis, Texas.

Jack spent most of the next week in Los Angeles. We saw each other nearly every day. I remember the two of us strap-hanging on a crowded city bus, entertaining the other passengers with a spontaneous comedy routine. I recall hiking in Griffith Park under the "Hollywoodland" sign. When I sang "Indian Love Call," a tenor voice from across the valley echoed the song. From then on, whenever Jack introduced me to his friends, he always added, proudly, "Mary's a *singer*." Except that he pronounced

my name "*May*-ry." I was nuts about that Texas accent.
And soon I was crazy about Jack Lummus.

One of the songs Annabelle Reinberg gave me to practice was a popular ballad of the year, "My Ideal."

> *Will I ever find the boy in my mind,*
> *The boy who is my ideal?*

I had found my ideal. But he wasn't a boy. He was a
man, so secure in his maturity that he enjoyed playing like
a boy. He cracked jokes and then laughed at them. He
razzed me about Nebraska's Cornhuskers and laughed at
my outrage. He poked fun at my deadly serious, Yankee
opinions. I puzzled for years over our arguments about
civil rights. Then I uncovered his friendship with Lonzo
Fields, a baseball player from the Negro League. I finally
realized that Jack had been kidding me, that he got a kick
out of raising my hackles. Yet, he "played" with the same
youthful joy and grace he displayed on the ball field. He
was never mean.

Mother and I always chuckled about Jack's comments
on Christmas Eve. Nancy and some of my roommates had
called up the U.S.O. and invited four lonesome servicemen to the house for turkey. When Jack came by to take
me out to dinner, he stood in the dining room archway
and looked at the group around the table.

"Two swab jockeys and a couple of dog faces," he said
matter-of-factly. His words remain a family joke.

We left the house and went to a dinner-dance at the
exclusive Coconut Grove in downtown Los Angeles. I
remember dancing in Jack's arms. I remember looking up

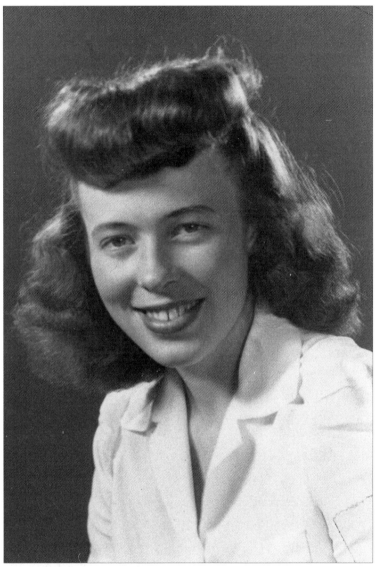

Posing for a studio portrait, the author was stiff and self-conscious. "Think of your sweetheart," the photographer suggested. Seconds later he caught the grin and sparkle in her eyes as she thought of Jack Lummus.

at his face, which by then I considered handsome. I remember my surprise and pleasure as we glided across the ballroom floor. For so tall a man, he was incredibly graceful.

After years of hindsight, I finally saw what happened to me that night. For the first time in my 19 years, I experienced adult emotions toward another human being. Before, I had been a girl attracted to a tall, handsome, fun-loving Texan. But that night the gulf between a girl's infatuation and a woman's deeper emotions disappeared. Can a person grow up in a week or two? An hour or two? I believe so. On that dance floor, I took a long step toward womanhood. I began to truly care for Jack, to fall in love with the man I had begun to know.

The war cheated Jack and me, as it did all couples, out of a traditional courtship. Nobody had time for orthodox love and marriage. Troopships loomed beside every dock. Death hovered a few days west of the coastline. Separations were inevitable; they would be long and limitless. Navy couples were better off because sailors returned Stateside whenever their ships did. Marines and Army men came home only if they received severe wounds. If they came home at all.

Emotions exploded. Romance sizzled. The pressures of war compressed months into weeks, weeks into days, days into hours. Couples made impulsive decisions.

Jack and I didn't have a chance to carry on long probing conversations. We didn't discover each other's favorite food, pet peeve, sports hero, movie star. Feelings about

God. Dreams. We let Frank Sinatra and Dinah Shore sing
our songs. "Besame Mucho," "People Will Say We're in
Love," "All or Nothing at All."

We listened to those songs, held hands to them,
danced to them. Then by New Year's Eve, two weeks into
our courtship, he said the magic words. "I love you, May-
ry." Never before had a boy or man spoken to me of love.
Not even my father, whose love I had never doubted.

That night, Jack and I talked about getting married. He
phoned my mother. She objected to our marrying right
then. Jack was sure to be sent overseas, she reminded
him. I was too young. She doubted I could handle it if he
got killed or came back maimed. She swept the decision
out of our hands.

Nancy and I had often argued before, and I had gotten
angry with her many times—when she left my father, for
instance. But I had never been as furious as I was that
night. Nor as hurt. It felt like she had reached through the
telephone line and skinned off the fragile veneer of adult-
hood I had so recently developed. She had stripped away
my rights to decide what I wanted of life. And she had
done it as casually as if she had been deciding what to
cook for supper.

But Jack had told me he loved me. And so, married or
not, we were committed.

When Jack took over his first command, we had to
snatch time together. I would ride the bus down to San
Clemente on a Saturday afternoon. That evening, we par-
tied with other couples. "She's a Rice girl," Jack would

say, introducing me to an officer's wife. Or about some-one else, "She's from Waxahachie." We formed congo lines and snaked through the halls of San Clemente's small hotel. We sang, "He's a ramblin' wreck from Georgia Tech" to one of Jack's buddies.

The parties and the impression of gaiety helped the Marines and their wives cope with what lay ahead: tomorrow and certain separation; tomorrow with its specter of death. It was a dreadful time for people in love.

Sunday afternoons, we swam in the wintry Pacific Ocean. Then we lay in the sun on the pleasant, almost deserted beach. Jack would hug me. "I cain't he'p it, May-ry," he would say, "I just love you."

In February, Jack went to Ennis on leave. He came up to Los Angeles to catch the train. On an impulse, he asked me to go home with him. At first, I said I couldn't; then I thought about it and decided I would go. But there wasn't time for me to get ready before his train left.

I have always been sad that the visit to his family didn't work out. For decades, I longed to meet Jack's family. When it became so very important that I go see them, I realized I didn't know his sisters' married names. I didn't know how to reach them. I didn't know how much Jack had told them about me. But finally, I didn't know how easy it would have been to locate them.

If only we had had more time. Time. The enemy of wartime love....

CHAPTER THIRTEEN

THE LAST GOODBYE

Combat training at Camp Pendleton swung into high gear during the spring and early summer of 1944. Jack Lummus suspected that the tough drills meant the Fifth Marine Division would soon board ships bound for the Pacific.

He didn't know, however, exactly where the Fifth Division would engage in its first battle. That had been decided in September 1943 when the military commanders in Washington, D.C., drew plans for the Fifth's venture. The Fifth would join the Third and Fourth Marine divisions to attack a force of 20,000 Japanese occupying an island called Iwo Jima. Under Lt. Gen. Tadamichi Kuribayashi, the troops there guarded the gateway to Tokyo Bay. Because the island lay just 660 miles from Tokyo, the operation would be daring and dangerous. It had to be kept strictly secret.

The troops prepared for the tough job ahead. Jack and the other company leaders put their men through a series of maneuvers that closely resembled the real battles they would face. Every acre of Pendleton echoed with the crack of weapons, some as small as pistols, others as large as mortars. Trainees soon learned to distinguish the sound of each weapon.

Because the Japanese often attacked after dark, Jack took his troops on night exercises at least six hours a week. In darkness and under fire, they crawled on their bellies 100 yards through barbed wire. They learned the value of helmets as protection against tracer bullets arcing overhead. During three-day bivouacs, they countered surprise infiltrations. They fired bazookas at tanks and slapped TNT-filled satchels onto pillboxes. They ran in front of the tanks, guiding them through tall grass, or alongside them, using the bulky vehicles as screens from sniper fire. They learned to string wire from post to outpost, to fire machine guns, to perform all jobs so as to replace fallen buddies.

Jack arranged for a gunnery sergeant to teach his company bayonet fighting. The instructor, John Whipple recalled, had spent more time in the brig than out of it. The "gunny" assumed a boxer's stance and sparred about with his bayonet. Keep your balance, he told them. Go for exposed skin, such as the fingers or ankles. "The minute the point of the weapon strikes blood, the adversary will look down at it. That's when you lunge at him, and not before."

From what Jack had heard, modern Marines didn't often fight with bayonets. Still, he wanted his men at least to know the technique.

As strenuous and tiring as the training was for his men in Company F, it was just as exhausting for Jack. Even so, he still found time for sports. I watched him play football at San Diego Stadium one Sunday. Without a program, I didn't realize that I might have been watching some of the nation's best college and professional players. During that period, Jack rubbed shoulders with some famous pro football players. They included Leroy Hirsch, Clipper Smith, Cliff Battles, Jack Chevniegh, Ray Apolskis, Bob Dove, Frank Hodges, and Bill Kennedy. Representing the Giants, besides Jack, were Frank Reagan and Orville Tuttle.

When he wasn't catching passes from the professionals, Jack often rounded up volunteers from his company for games of touch football. The games usually pitted officers against enlisted men.

"We played evenings when we didn't have night maneuvers. We played on weekends when we pulled the duty," explained Ted Johnson, an enlisted man from Company F. "We were a close-knit outfit, a lot closer than the rest of the Corps." Close friends or not, they played rough and tackled dirty. Although they wore very little padding, the men wound up with bumps and bruises but no serious injuries. Johnson felt as if he had done something really special when he tackled Jack. "A player of his caliber was a tough adversary. But we all loved him."

"There were never any grudges," Johnson claimed. "After the games, we would go back to being Marines as if nothing had happened."

Dr. Thomas M. Brown, surgeon for the Twenty-seventh's Second Battalion, noted that Jack's great easy strides looked like they were a foot or two above ground. "He was as graceful as a gazelle at top speed," said Dr. Brown.

The games ceased when Jack received a telegram from home. Andrew Jackson Lummus, an Ennis police officer, had been shot and killed on May 13, 1944. Jack requested emergency leave and flew to Dallas.

Jack arrived in Ennis to find the townspeople expecting him to wreak revenge on Olin Mount, his father's murderer. Word had spread that Jack commanded a company of vicious Marine commandos. Commandos, folks whispered, would just as soon slit your throat as look at you.

People hung around street corners or loafed at lunch counters. They sipped coffee and rehashed events that had led up to the shooting of "Happy Jack" Lummus.

A. J. Lummus and Olin Mount had spent that fateful May night together, lounging around a cafe, sipping whiskey. Happy Jack worked as constable for the City of Ennis; Mount was special agent, or detective, for the Southern Pacific Railroad. The two had known each other a long time. Sometimes they assisted each other making arrests; once in a while they cooperated to solve a crime. Both carried pistols.

Just like his son, Happy Jack enjoyed teasing. Nothing

tickled him more than to "get a rise" out of someone, especially someone he liked. But that Saturday evening, the joke backfired. A. J. had been kidding Mount about a nurse. As night cops, Lummus and Mount took turns picking up the night nurse at the hospital when she came off duty. Ennis didn't have streetcars or buses or even taxicabs, so they drove her home.

Giving a nurse a ride seems like a simple errand of mercy. But Olin Mount grew angry when Happy Jack teased him about it. Maybe Mount, a married man, had a crush on her. Maybe he was just in a foul mood. Or maybe the razzing along with all the liquor he had consumed combined to inflame the small man. Whatever the reason, Mount became agitated and jumped to his feet. Yanking out his revolver, he fired point blank at his tormentor. The bullet exploded in Happy Jack's stomach. He died instantly.

The crime incensed the townspeople. For 20 years, the friendly, "funning" A. J. Lummus had served the citizens of Ellis County faithfully. Everyone liked him.

So when Jack showed up, the town's citizens wondered how the boy would react to his father's senseless death.

It didn't take long for Jack to answer them. He marched into the mortuary, his back razor-straight, his chin squared. He walked up to his father's casket and stared down for a moment. Then he saluted. Every mourner in the place sighed.

The family arrived at the church, their sorrow at such a

great loss lining their faces. A. J.'s daughters, his sons-in-law, his grandchildren sat in a hurt silence around Laura, A. J.'s widow.

Jack was the rock that supported his mother on the agonizing ride to Myrtle Cemetery. They interred Andrew Jackson Lummus in the family plot next to his brother, Sye, who had died of pneumonia in the First World War.

The next day, Jack retained a lawyer to look into Laura's finances and keep an eye on the prosecution of Olin Mount. At Waxahachie some time later, an Ellis County jury convicted Mount of murder. The judge, rather than incarcerating an old man in the penitentiary, placed him on probation. Two years later, Mount committed suicide.

Laura and Thelma watched Jack pack his bag for the return trip to California. They hated to have him leave. When would they see him again? When would he be sent overseas? Laura asked what he planned to do after the war ended. Jack said he'd probably be too old to play professional ball by then. "I've been thinking about making a career in the Marine Corps," he said.

Thelma asked if he ever thought about getting married. "I've got someone out in California," he told her. But he felt it wouldn't be fair to marry her, in case he didn't come back. "Or came back all shot up."

Ready to leave, Jack hugged his mother. "Don't worry, Mom," he said. "I'll always take care of you."

Upon his return to Camp Pendleton, Jack found the

war news encouraging. Four hundred thousand American and British soldiers crossed the English Channel and shoved the Germans back from the French coast. On the other side of the world, the Second and Fourth Marine divisions fought crack Japanese troops on Saipan. Nearly 3,500 Americans died in that battle. One of them was Jack Lummus' friend and former Camp Elliott baseball teammate, Jack Casey.

Meanwhile, action at Pendleton grew increasingly hectic as the Fifth Division got ready for war. Both the date they would ship out and the location of the island they would invade were still closely guarded secrets.

In early July, all three of the Fifth's regiments boarded transports. They left the California coast and sailed 60 miles across the Gulf of Santa Catalina. Reaching barren San Clemente Island, they climbed down rope nets and waded through the surf. As though attacking an enemy stronghold, they "assaulted" the island. Then they reboarded their ships and sailed back to Oceanside. This time, the Twenty-seventh and Twenty-eighth regiments assaulted the beaches north of Camp Pendleton's main gate. Defending the mainland was the Twenty-sixth Regiment. Communiques identified this target as "Pendleton Island, a strongly held Japanese airbase in the West Pacific."

Officials from various Allied countries came to observe the maneuvers. They represented the British Royal Marines, Royal Netherlands Marines, and the Royal Canadian Army and Navy. There were officers from

Australia and New Zealand, and even a Free French military mission.

On July 11, 1944, a big black limousine pulled up. Observing the maneuvers from inside the car were President Franklin Delano Roosevelt and his son, Elliott. Before the president and Elliott left, they presented the Fifth Division with a mascot, their Saint Bernard dog.

Nobody had time to exercise the dog, however, for the training became even more intense. Maneuvers and forced marches ran all night sometimes.

Then it became apparent that more and more Marines were taking advantage of the hubbub to sneak out of camp and go home. Scared and homesick, a lowly private watched until his preoccupied superior officer turned his back. Then the Marine deserted. He avoided train and bus stations where military police might ask to see his travel orders. If he was lucky, he found his way home and hid out. Eventually, though, the MPs came looking for him. If they found him—and they usually did—they put him in chains and escorted him to the federal prison at Fort Leavenworth, Kansas.

The commanders of the Fifth Division discussed the crisis and agreed they had to do something. The invasion of Iwo Jima wouldn't take place for several months, not until February 1945. If they merely ignored the situation and looked the other way, the number of desertions would increase.

"A decision came down from Washington to ship the entire Fifth Division to the Big Island of Hawaii," said

William Eslinger. It would be a lot harder for a runaway Marine to find his way home across 2,000 miles of Pacific Ocean. Eslinger, by then, had received a promotion to chief clerk typist and had transferred out of Fox Company to Second Battalion headquarters. Placed under strict security protection, he started to type the multitude of orders that would move the entire division to Hawaii.

On July 12, the Fifth's commanders again sent the Twenty-seventh and Twenty-eighth regiments across the Gulf of Santa Catalina to "attack" San Clemente Island. Back at the base, the Twenty-sixth Regiment started packing. Soon, they were in San Diego boarding ships. On July 26, the convoy sailed out of San Diego Bay. Destination: Hawaii.

Within two weeks, Jack's Twenty-seventh Regiment had started to mark and pack and crate its equipment.

Up in Los Angeles, I didn't know what was going on at Pendleton. I did know that I didn't see Jack as often as I'd like. I knew he was busy, of course. I knew he would be shipping overseas soon. But as my love for him grew stronger and deeper, I had to find a way to spend more time with him.

My boss gave me the afternoon off. I called Jack at Pendleton and asked him to meet me at the end of the Pacific Electric streetcar line. Jack borrowed a car and came to pick me up. That's the only time I ever saw him

Photo of Jack Lummus in dungarees, taken probably at Camp Pendleton.
(Courtesy Sue Merritt)

wearing dungarees.

We sat in the car, talking. I recall staring out the windshield at a gray world: a dismal gray sky and a pewter-colored ocean.

This time, Jack didn't tease me. We didn't laugh and joke or clown around. We didn't even argue. It was our most serious conversation to date.

"Please, Jack, let's get married," I begged. "Let's be together for however long you've got left."

My timing, of course, couldn't have been worse. It had been such a short time since his father's death. I can guess at the thoughts that rushed through his mind: How could he take a wife right then when he had promised his mother he would take care of her? How could he assign his allotment and insurance to a wife when his mother needed it worse? What if we conceived a child before he left?

He didn't say any of that. What he did was repeat the reasoning he had given Thelma, the reasons my mother had handed him on New Year's Eve: What if he died? What if he came back all shot up?

That wouldn't matter, I pleaded. I loved *him,* not an arm or leg. I would always love him. No matter what.

I had dumped a cruel puzzle in his lap, and I couldn't budge him. Feeling frustrated and sad, I returned to Los Angeles.

When I didn't hear from him in the next two weeks, I began to feel rejected and angry. I knew nothing of the flurry of activity going on at Camp Pendleton. The regiment was packing. They placed every piece of equipment, large and small, into boxes. They stenciled two code names on each box: one for the regiment's destination, the other for the ship they would board. In a few days, Camp Pendleton resembled a huge outdoor warehouse with crates piled everywhere. Trucks pulled in and the Marines packed them with boxes. In the final days, loading parties worked round the clock, not even stopping to eat. With the last crate placed on the last truck, the men of the Twenty-seventh went to their tents and packed personal gear.

Finally, more trucks arrived, and the two-day exodus began. Thousands of Marines and every piece of their equipment left for San Diego.

Then in the middle of the night of August 11, 1944, one of my roommates shouted up the stairs. Jack was calling. He wanted to come to North Hollywood and pick me up. I should have realized how important the call was, for he had never before phoned in the middle of the night. Instead, it rattled me.

"Call me in the morning," I said. Jack pleaded; he

almost begged. "Call me in the morning," I repeated stubbornly. I was half asleep; but I was still half mad that he had spurned my proposal two weeks earlier.

If Jack could have told me why he was calling... but he couldn't. When a Marine unit prepared to ship out, they placed the men on alert and swore them to secrecy. Jack's sense of honor wouldn't allow him to break that vow of secrecy.

So we said goodbye and hung up. I never went back to bed. Without turning on the lights, I sat in the dark living room, staring out the front window at the empty street. Wishing Jack would ignore my refusal and drive up.

I kicked myself. Why didn't I have enough confidence in Jack to realize that he had a sound reason for calling so late?

At dawn, I tried to reach him at the base. No one would, or could, tell me where he was. After several attempts, I gave up.

Too drained to go to work, I spent the morning hunting for my roommate's dog. He had run off. I walked all over the neighborhood, crying and calling, "Here, Mike. Here, Mike." It wasn't the dog I called. It wasn't the dog I cried for.

That weekend, Lois and Marie and I moved to a small house in Glendale. Mother had moved to San Francisco.

A few days later, the mailman brought a letter from Jack, the first he'd ever written me. The envelope carried a San Diego postmark. By then, Jack's ship was at sea.

"There's a lot of plans I have for the two of us when I

get back," he wrote.

Reading his farewell note made me sadder. Now instead of being angry at Jack, I was angry at myself. Had I gone with him, had we spent those last hours together, he would have shared those plans with me. I would have heard the words from his lips, from his heart. I so badly needed to hear those words. I would have gone to San Diego and stood on the dock. I would have waved at his ship until I could no longer see its shape on the ocean.

We would have said a proper goodbye.

CHAPTER FOURTEEN

HAWAIIAN SUNSETS

The shouts of longshoremen echoed up and down the San Diego docks. Winches screeched as cranes lifted equipment aboard the troop transports. Columns of Marines snaked up gangways, helmets on their heads and field packs on their backs. At first opportunity, they dumped their heavy seabags on the deck.

Jack Lummus stood at the top of the USS *Henry Clay's* gangway, checking off the names Marines called as they trudged past.

At 2100 on Saturday, August 12, 1944, the *Henry Clay* cast off her moorings and eased away from the dock. The skipper maneuvered behind the long line of troopships streaming out of the harbor into San Diego Bay. As the last ship cleared the channel, submarine nets closed behind its bow. The troopships moved into position between the destroyers and light cruisers, their armor against attack. The convoy turned west and settled into a zigzag pattern intended to elude an enemy submarine's torpedoes.

Jack signed the roster and handed it to the captain. Then he scrambled down ladders to the second deck below waterline. There he found Marines crowded into damp, murky compartments, two forward and two aft.

Boys on their first sea voyage had jumbled packs, helmets, knapsacks, seabags, and shovels onto their bunks. Veterans who had sailed on troopships before stowed their gear in the aisle. The aisle was so narrow and crowded that Jack had to turn sideways to get through.

A deafening announcement blared from loudspeakers: "Sweepers, man your brooms. A clean sweep-down, fore and aft."

Jack pulled out his handkerchief and wiped sweat from his face. The heat was stifling, and the "canned" air that swished from the ventilators did little to cool the hold.

It was past midnight but the loudspeaker continued to blare: orders for cooks and messboys to "lay below" to the galley.

Some of the Marines had stripped off their shirts and crawled into their bunks. In the dim light, they squinted at paperbacks or dog-eared magazines. They reread old, crinkled letters from home. After a while, they just stared into space, thinking about those they left behind, dreading what lay ahead. Bunks consisted of canvas rectangles laced to frames and fastened to the bulkhead by ropes or chains. With the bunks five and six tiers deep, a man trying to sleep had to lie flat on his back or stomach. If he turned on his side, his shoulder and hip banged into the bunk above.

Many gave up on bunks and, squatting where they could, wrote letters home. Others gabbed with buddies, played gin rummy, or cleaned rifles. One grizzled Marine honed his Kabar, a seven-inch fighting knife.

Jack crouched beside a bunk, talking quietly with a homesick kid. They prayed together, and he went on down the aisle. He stopped beside a boy whose face had turned chalky white. Seasick, he figured. The farther the *Clay* steamed from shore, the rougher the California swells that rocked it. He sent the Marine up to sickbay. Other Marines wanted to talk about the rumors they'd heard. Was it a fact that they were headed for San Francisco? Naw, not true, said another Marine. "I heard it on good authority that we're going straight to the Kurile Islands, just north of Japan." Jack assured the boys that he didn't believe either rumor.

Finally, Jack left and went to his bunk in the clean, roomy quarters he shared with three other officers. He slept but a short time when an announcement over the loudspeaker awoke him: "Abandon-ship drill." He clawed through his gear and found his Mae West flotation vest. He went on deck for the drill.

Their second day at sea, a Sunday, Jack went down into the hold again. He invited the enlisted men to the top deck for worship services. As the chaplain began his sermon, a dog ran through the crowd. A second dog chased him. Then Jack saw several dogs scampering around. They were pets that Marines had smuggled aboard in crates and seabags. "How you think you gonna get that mongrel past quarantine?" Jack heard a sergeant bellow at a Marine.

On Monday, the August weather turned hot. The Marines that weren't seasick went to the top deck to catch the breeze. There wasn't much for them to do. Jeeps and crates of equipment, chained and roped to stanchions, took up most of the deck space. There wasn't enough room left over to do calisthenics or hold inspections. Some of the more inventive, however, turned hatch covers into boxing rings and promoted matches.

Men lounged around, reading whodunits or watching for flying fish. They kibitzed as sailors test-fired their 20mm guns at targets towed by radio-controlled planes. They drank gallons of coffee and played cribbage or poker. Most, though, milled around, waiting in lines. They lined up to shower and shave in distilled water. They queued up for sickbay or the soda fountain, for the library or a crewcut at the barber's. They wedged into endless chains for the heads or the galleys.

Messboys served two light meals a day. Chow lines were so long that by the time a man bolted down lunch, standing up, it was time to fall in again for supper.

Evenings, some of the Marines leaned on rails, gazing at the quarter moon, talking about home, wives, sweethearts. When night fell, they had to go below. Convoy security required that all ships be blacked out, and the Navy banned Marines from the top deck. They either sprawled onto their bunks or filed into the messhalls to watch movies.

Well out to sea, Jack put a stop to the rumors by briefing the enlisted men. A loud cheer rang out when he told them they were headed for Camp Tarawa on the island of Hawaii. Native Hawaiians called it the Big Island, he explained, because it was twice as large as all the other Hawaiian islands combined. There they would rejoin the Twenty-sixth Regiment that had left Pendleton two weeks earlier.

"All you can tell the folks back home is that you're on an island somewhere in the Pacific," Jack warned. From then on, censors would read their letters. "Any mention of pineapples, sugar cane, or hula skirts will be blacked out or cut out," he said.

After six days at sea, sailors on the *Henry Clay* sighted the island of Oahu. Marines stared in horror as the convoy steamed past the wrecked hulls of Navy ships at Pearl Harbor. Several hours later, the *Clay* rounded a stone breakwater. It nosed into Hilo Bay and up to a dock at the village of Hilo.

The "seagoing bellhops," as sailors called Marines, unloaded their equipment. They boarded trucks, small landing craft, and railway boxcars and headed up the mountains to the towns of Kamuela and Kona. There, camp headquarters snuggled up to the foothills of Mauna

Jack Lummus pictured in front of his tent during the Fifth Division's bivouac at Camp Tarawa on Hawaii before shipping out for Iwo Jima. (Courtesy Richard A. Tilghman)

Dressed in dungarees, Jack Lummus and his buddies posed for a picture while the Fifth Marine Division was at Camp Tarawa, Hawaii. From left, Don Hendricks, Cliff Fulcher, Oscar Gray, Jack Lummus, and Bill McCann. (Courtesy Bill McCann)

Kea, the 14,000-foot-high volcano.

North of Kona lay Parker Ranch, the second largest ranch in the world. Its 225,000 acres spread over 40 or 50 miles. The King Ranch in Texas, at 823,000 acres, was the world's largest ranch. After the Japanese attacked Pearl Harbor, the U. S. Navy leased Parker Ranch for one dollar. They named it Camp Tarawa to honor Second Division Marines who died fighting the Japanese for the island of Tarawa.

Camp Tarawa was quite primitive. A few wood and caneboard structures were used for administration offices. Farther along, Quonset huts served as storerooms and galleys. Officers and enlisted men lived back in a desolate area. Their quarters consisted of pyramid-shaped tents pitched over shaky wooden decks.

The days were warm, often rainy, and always windy. The nights were cold, made even colder by strong, wet winds that blew down from the snowcapped Kohala Mountains. Jack's tent rocked 24 hours a day in the constant gusts.

The camp was laid out over a flat outcropping of lava. Six inches of a powdery, unstable, ancient lava dust covered the ground. The blowing lava dust choked the men. Worse, moisture in the winds saturated the airborne soil. A thick, mud-colored plaster coated faces, dungarees, rifles, tents.

By the time the regiment settled in, Jack no longer commanded Company F. Maj. John Antonelli, Jack's good friend and commander of the Second Battalion, had reassigned Jack as chief of the battalion's message center.

Jack also made friends with Capt. Bill McCann, commanding officer of Company E. They had college and professional sports careers in common. McCann had played varsity baseball and basketball for the University of Virginia; after graduating, he played one season as an All-Star second baseman with a Class C club.

"Many times, Jack and I played touch football, volleyball, and so on," McCann recalled. Although Jack was no longer commander of Company F, he often saw the Marines from his former company.

"You guys want to play some touch football?" he would ask Wayne Dust or Hardy Brown. Soon, he had enough officers and enlisted men to make up a couple of teams. Off they would go, to the athletic fields at Parker Ranch or Maume Beach, or to the battalion parade grounds.

William Wick described the games as "often quite rough," the line-ups "always informal." Sometimes Jack would put officers on one team, enlisted men on the other; other times, each team might have privates and sergeants, lieutenants and captains.

Wick recalled a game when he and Jack were on the same team: they had the ball and went into huddle to call a new play. Jack looked at Wick and said, "Billy, you run down the right sideline, long, and I'll drop it in to you." Wick followed orders, and Jack passed the ball about 50 yards. Wick caught it, outran the tacklers, and scored a touchdown. "What a pass!" Wick exclaimed.

Trying to block a man of Jack's size, his speed, and his experience, frustrated some of the players. Milo Urdesich, a private first class, remembered when his team was playing, officers against enlisted men. "I was halfback, and my job was to block Jack." Urdesich tried, but Jack was intent on rushing after the ball carrier. "Well, he went through me like I wasn't even there," Urdesich said. Urdesich did manage to block Jack once when he fell in front of him and accidentally tripped him.

Pete Piesik—only five feet eight to Jack's six-four—swore Jack could snag a pass 12 feet in the air. Maybe

higher. "Jack was very competitive," Piesik said.

In one game, Jack caught a pass right in front of Wayne Dust. "He turned and headed for the goal, and I went down like I'd been hit by a truck," Dust recalled. "Jack had such a strong desire to win."

When he wasn't playing football or handling his duties at the message center, Jack went to the beach. He and Lt. Richard Tilghman, a Fox Company platoon leader, found the fish at Kona Beach some of the

Jack Lummus posed with a fish he caught with a blast of TNT at Maume Beach along the west coast of the Big Island of Hawaii. (Courtesy Bill McCann)

best on the island. "We used to take our catch back to the mess for the officers and enlisted men," Tilghman said.

Bill McCann recalled weekends that he and Jack and Don Hendricks piled into jeeps and drove to Maume Beach. "We would catch fish with half-pound blocks of TNT. Then we'd fry them with potatoes and onions," McCann said. "Terrific!"

Around the first of September, the Twenty-eighth Regiment arrived. With all three regiments on the island, softball and baseball teams formed. Games were scheduled between the division and its three regiments, and between all units under them. Tournaments were initiated, and "Baseball today" signs went up at the Kamuela diamond.

Thousands of Marines cheered when the Fifth Division's "Sluggers" went against touring teams. The road teams consisted of major and minor league baseball stars who had joined the armed forces. Capt. Harry Maynard's idea for the Devildogs had finally caught on.

Jack wore jersey number 14 when he covered first base for the Twenty-seventh Regiment's team. Bill McCann played second base. In early November, Jack's ball club went against the Twenty-eighth Regiment's team for the division championship. "I don't remember the score," McCann said, "but the Twenty-seventh took the title."

By then, most of the Fifth Division's support troops either had settled in at Camp Tarawa or were on the way. The Thirteenth Artillery Regiment arrived in October. In

December, the rest of the support troops arrived. Those included the dog platoons and Army Signal Aircraft Warning units. Black troops from the Army's 471st Amphibian Truck Company brought in the new DUKWs. DUKWs were a strange breed of motor vehicle. They were either boats that could travel on land or trucks that could motor through the ocean.

With the Fifth Division's full complement in place, fun and games, championship tournaments, dynamite fishing, touch football, all were about to come to a screeching halt.

CHAPTER FIFTEEN

ON THEIR WAY

For a year, the president's military advisers in Washington, D.C., had been arguing. The Joint Chiefs of Staff were involved in a power struggle between the Army's Gen. Douglas MacArthur and the Navy's Adm. Chester W. Nimitz. MacArthur wanted the Fifth Marine Division to attack the island of Formosa. Driving the Japanese off Formosa would help MacArthur recapture the Philippines. Nimitz argued for Iwo Jima. In a few weeks, B-29 Superfortresses and B-24 Liberators would lift off Saipan and start their daily bombing runs to Tokyo. En route, they would fly over Iwo. On their way back to Saipan, some of the bombers might be crippled from anti-aircraft fire. Or they might have engine trouble. The bombers would be especially vulnerable to attack by

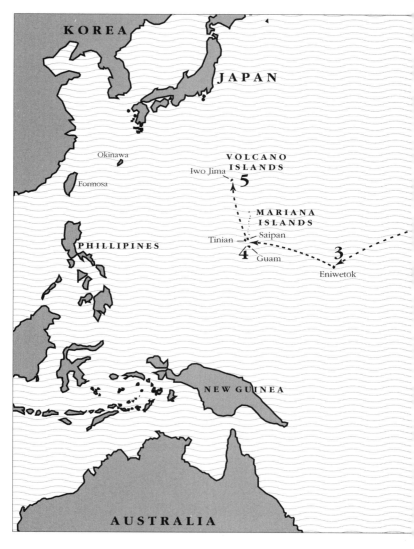

1. *San Diego. Jack Lummus left August 12, 1944 aboard* USS *Henry Clay and arrived six days later at the "Big Island" of Hawaii.*

2. *Honolulu. The Fourth and Fifth Divisions left Hawaii on January 27, 1945.*

3. *Eniwetok. The 800 ship convoy arrived February 5, 1945 and left two days later.*

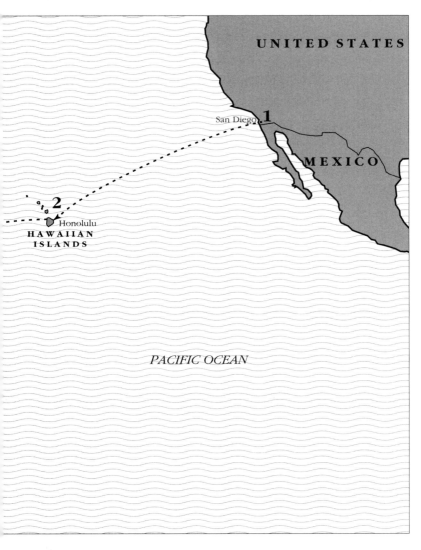

4. *Saipan, Tinian, Guam. The ships arrived February 11 at Saipan in the Marianas. The next day they sailed to Tinian for maneuvers. The Third Marine division sailed up from Guam to join the other two divisions for the invasion of Iwo Jima.*
5. *Iwo Jima. The huge convoy arrived off Iwo Jima's shores on February 17, 1945. The invasion began early in the morning two days later.*

Japanese fighter planes and would need Iwo's two airstrips for emergency landings.

Nimitz won the argument. On October 3, 1944, the council scrapped the Formosa plan and told Maj. Gen. Keller E. Rockey to get the Fifth Division ready to leave Camp Tarawa by the end of 1944. Training and exercises sped up.

While the Marines on Hawaii fought mock battles, the Japanese general, Kuribayashi, continued to fortify Iwo Jima's unusual defenses. He directed his laborers to dig deep holes in the island's loose volcanic sand. In the holes, they buried such heavy weapons as antiaircraft guns, rockets, and mortars. They even buried entire tanks. All that showed were slits or gun ports for the barrels. At strategic locations, Kuribayashi built clusters of pillboxes and connected them through underground tunnels and trenches.

Kuribayashi didn't billet his troops in ground-level tents or buildings as Americans did. He blasted underground rooms out of the volcanic rock. One-room units housed only a few troops. Some went down two stories. A few were four stories deep and held 300 or 400 troops. Each room had more than one entrance and exit and was connected to other rooms by stairways and tunnels. Some of these passageways ran the entire length of the island and were lit by electric lights, oil lamps, or candles.

While Kuribayashi prepared for the invasion, Marines on Hawaii prepared to invade. The sprawling, 10-square-mile range around Kamuela bustled both day and night.

Marines rehearsed jungle tactics in the forested area that stretched toward the mountains. In the rolling lava fields, they perfected foxhole-digging techniques. They marched up and down the 12-mile trail south of Parker Ranch. A former Olympic champion swimmer, Melvin Archer, took over a clear-water lagoon and taught Marines to swim.

Commanders scaled small rises to observe their troops practicing maneuvers under real artillery fire. Dr. Tom Brown and other doctors staffed first-aid stations and the Army hospital at Kamuela. Engineers repaired Camp Tarawa's old buildings or erected new ones. Motor transport units hauled supplies between Hilo and Kamuela. Seabees drilled in combat procedures. Service companies provided fuel, clothing, shoe repair, and laundry. Cooks prepared meals with dehydrated food. And language officers lectured Marines on Japanese phrases. Overhead, single-passenger cub planes flew reconnaissance.

Combat units boarded amphibious tractors, called "amtracs" that, similar to DUKWs, traveled on land or sea. They practiced making amphibious landings with different combinations of infantrymen, tanks, artillery, and engineers. Over and over, they drilled on what to do *after* they landed. "We kept attacking an area on the beach called 'Island X,'" explained Sgt. Jack Carns. He thought it odd that after every landing, they immediately turned right.

Carns also thought it odd when he spotted a Navy aerial photograph in the *Honolulu Advertiser* one day. It was a picture of bombs falling from B-24 Liberators that were based in the Marianas. Lines under the photo identified the target as Iwo Jima, an island south of Japan. The island's shape reminded Carns of "Island X." When none of his superiors commented about the similarity, Carns shrugged it off.

One who didn't shrug anything off was Staff Sgt. William Eslinger, chief clerk typist for the Twenty-seventh Regiment's Second Battalion. Eslinger, who had a high security clearance, was placed under armed guard just before Christmas. His superior officers brought in top-secret information and ordered him to type it up. What he was typing, Eslinger soon realized, was invasion orders. It wouldn't be long before the Fifth Division got back on their ships. But not even Sergeant Eslinger knew where the Fifth would be going.

With the paperwork rolling out of Eslinger's typewriter, the maneuvers suddenly took on a different air. No longer did the Marines "play" soldier out on a practice field. Now they turned to the serious business of fighting on a "battle-field."

Majors and captains operated command posts. They issued combat orders, compiled records, and wrote reports. Lieutenants pitted their men against each other in the hand-to-hand clashes the Japanese preferred. Platoon and squad leaders memorized where each individual in their units must be at all times. Leaders also learned to perform every task done by every man in their units.

The generals and admirals anticipated a large number

of casualties when the Fifth Division invaded Iwo Jima. They directed officers and noncoms to take turns leading their units. If a platoon leader was killed or wounded, for instance, the sergeant must be schooled to take over the lieutenant's responsibilities. A private first class must be able to replace his corporal or sergeant.

In the final phase of training, General Rockey and his staff watched the Fifth prepare to practice amphibious landings for three days and nights. It felt so real that Jack's heart raced as he and his radio operators climbed into their amphibious tractor. They were part of a combat team made up of infantrymen, staff officers, engineers, tanks, and mechanized weapons.

Then with fighter planes and dive bombers flying over-head, Jack's amtrac plowed through the surf. Once again Jack and his men landed on the beach. Once again, the Fifth attacked "Island X." Once again, the Twenty-seventh Regiment turned right.

Next, the amtracs took the Marines to Hilo. Jack's vehicle chugged up to an LST—a landing ship designed to carry tanks as well as men. Heavy radio packs on their backs, they climbed nets onto the LST's deck. Then they climbed back down into their bobbing amtracs.

On December 20, the Fifth Division returned to Camp Tarawa. Tough Marines cringed and turned white as medics came at them with large hypodermic needles. The shots immunized them against typhus, cholera, and the plague.

The feeling of being at war grew even greater when

quartermasters issued live ammunition and Marines received orders to load their rifles and pistols. Another order came down that each Marine must always be ready to show his credentials. If a sentry challenged him, he must know the day's password.

Make no mistake about it, Jack told himself. The Fifth Division would ship out right after the holidays.

On Christmas Eve, Jack probably relaxed by listening to the military's short-wave broadcast of the Mosquito Bowl football game on Guadalcanal. How he must have longed to be on the gridiron himself. I'd like to think that he also reminisced about our big date just the year before: the Christmas Eve dinner-dance; the night we started to fall in love. On Christmas Day, he stood among a sea of Marines listening to the Protestant chaplain's message of hope, his prayer that the Christ child would bring peace to the world.

Jack didn't hang around camp Christmas Day. He left the mail clerks busily distributing mountains of Christmas cards and packages. He walked away from the Marines wolfing down turkey and dressing in the mess halls. He didn't go to the officers' club to play gin rummy. Jack went to the Kona Coast's black-sand beach.

"I didn't want to go to town with the boys," he wrote his sister, Thelma. "I had a lot of thinking to do." Jack spent Christmas Day sitting on a large rock, watching the ocean.

Who can guess the channels Jack's mind wandered down that day? Heading for his first battle, he must have touched all the raw edges of his emotions. He surely revisited his fears, his hopes, his faith. No doubt his feelings seesawed between excitement and anxiety. It was worse than going up to bat in the ninth inning with the score tied and bases loaded.

During those lonely hours, he would have conjured up mental images of those he loved: his mother, his sisters, his nephew and niece. His ears must have rung with the laughter of the fun-loving father he'd lost just seven months before. And very likely his thoughts probed the confusing turn our romance had taken.

CHAPTER SIXTEEN

SEPARATION BLUES

When Jack shipped out of California, I was upset. No, I was angry. His abrupt departure left me feeling rejected and frustrated. I knew he had no choice but to get on that ship and go. Yet, did he have to leave without warning me, without preparing me, without saying good-bye? Then I would remind myself that he had tried to spend his last night with me. It was my own fault that he didn't; I could blame no one but myself. Feeling childish and selfish, I chastised myself: Maybe Mother was right. Maybe I *was* too young.

What should I do? What if I hopped a train and went to Ennis, Texas, and found Jack's family? At the age of 19, though, it seemed truly scary to go up to his mother and introduce myself.

Then the newspapers reported that the Fifth Division had gone to Hawaii. I thought about following him. In wartime, however, a civilian couldn't just jump on a ship and go to the islands. I considered auditioning for the United Service Organization. The U.S.O. took singers and musicians and comedians all over the world to entertain our boys in uniform. I doubted that I could insist on going to Hawaii. With my luck, I'd wind up in London, halfway around the world from the Fifth Marine Division.

I decided to go home and visit Dad for a while. Mother still lived in San Francisco, my brother was with Patton's army in France, and Dad was all alone. In one of my first letters to Jack, I asked if he thought I should go back to Nebraska. "You do what you want," he replied. "I know you will anyway." Ironically, one of my roommates forwarded that letter to me at Dad's house.

I spent three months in the war-forlorn small town I grew up in. Nearly all my high school friends had left. The boys were off firing bullets. The girls were firing rivets in defense plants.

So for 90 days, I moped around Dad's house, sunk in a blue mood I couldn't shake. Today a doctor would diagnose my condition as depression. It was difficult to write even a few lines to Jack. The ability to pick up a pen and compose warm, loving, optimistic letters had deserted me.

I went out a few times with a navigator from the Kearney Air Base, 25 miles north of Holdrege. He taught me to find the North Star and Orion and other constellations in the November sky. He came from Redwood City, California, and seemed like a pleasant young boy. But he wasn't Jack.

The situation evolved into a vicious circle. The less often I wrote Jack, the fewer letters he wrote me. Finally, we almost stopped writing each other. I'm sure Jack was disappointed. Worried, too. I was just numb.

Then along about mid-December, a revelation struck me like a bolt of lightning, like a religious conversion. *Why am I in Nebraska? I love Jack.* Anger left me. Indecision and depression vanished. I no longer argued with myself about what I wanted to do. More than anything in the world, I wanted to hurry back to the West Coast. I wanted to live as close to my love as possible.

On Christmas night, I rode the Pacific Electric train down to San Clemente. Down by the wharf, I sat on a patch of sand. If it wasn't the same spot where Jack and I had often soaked up the sun, it was at least close. But now it was dark. I stared at the ocean, stared west toward Hawaii, toward Jack. Suddenly, a bright star appeared in the black of the western sky. One of the planets, I guessed. Then I saw the star's brilliance mirrored on the combers of a gentle surf. The long track seemed like a filament reaching from the western horizon to my sandy sanctuary. An eerie wonder filled my heart with peace.

I didn't know about Jack's special rock on Kona Beach. I didn't know that he often sat there, waiting for the huge orange Hawaiian moon to rise. With luck, he'd catch sight of a rainbow, breathtakingly beautiful in the moonlight.

Especially that night, he would have stared across the

Pacific, reliving past Christmases with the family he loved so dearly. In my heart, I know he was also thinking of the girl he still pictured in Nebraska.

I must also believe that, despite the time difference of two and a half hours, Jack and I were staring toward each other.

CHAPTER SEVENTEEN

LAST DAYS AT PEARL HARBOR

All during the week between December 26, 1944, and New Year's Eve, Camp Tarawa bustled with activity. Thousands of Marines from the Fifth Division loaded their crated equipment into trucks. Then the Marines themselves jumped in, and the exodus began.

Sixty-five miles southeast at the port of Hilo, an armada of ships awaited the Marines. The USS *Highlands* arrived at Hilo on December 30. It joined the AKA *Athene*—a fast amphibious support ship—and a fleet of LSTs.

Day and night, trucks struggled up the steep slopes of the snow-peaked, dormant volcano, Mauna Kea. They ferried the bulk of the division across the Saddle Road and down to Hilo. Other convoys carried their loads up Highway 19 to the railhead where open flat cars waited. Trucks took Ted Johnson's unit 15 miles west of Kamuela to Kawaihae Bay where they boarded LST 715. By New Year's Eve, Camp Tarawa looked as deserted as Pendleton had four months earlier.

Military Police restricted the public's access to Hilo's beaches and docks as a steady stream of Marines arrived and boarded ships. Jack and his communications unit steamed out of Hilo Bay aboard LST 756.

About January 5, Jack stood at the rail of his LST as it sailed north, past the islands of Maui and Lanai and Molokai. Hours later the convoy skirted Hickam Air Base and slipped through submarine nets into the entrance to Pearl Harbor. Jack saw some of the debris that still remained from the Japanese bombs. He also saw destroyers and cruisers looking like toy models beside the enormous steel-gray carriers and battleships. He could have sworn the entire Pacific fleet was there.

Shortly after the ships carrying the Fifth arrived at Pearl Harbor, another armada arrived from Maui. Aboard were Fourth Division Marines. Word spread among the excited Marines that the Fourth would be going with the Fifth— wherever that might be.

On one of the ships, a sailor found five boxes of safety matches rolled in newspapers and tucked inside a cargo pallet. Someone had rearranged the matches' sulfur heads to scrape against each other and ignite. Suspecting sabotage, Military Police searched all ships and the entire dock area, looking for vandalism. Finding nothing, they decided that one of the sailors had pulled a prank. A fire-damaged ship would allow him a longer shore leave.

Meanwhile, gigs and landing craft sped between ships, churning the harbor into wakes of white foam. Oil tankers edged up to huge ships and fed in their hoses. Barges and tenders brought food and water out to the ships, as well as weapons and ammunition. The ships had to carry enough stores to support nearly 70,000 Marines and sailors during a long sea voyage and an island campaign. Hoping that no one noticed, the sailors quietly slipped white wooden crosses and other burial equipment into the holds.

Then the submarine nets parted again and the ships sailed out to sea. They turned south. "This is it! We're off to whip the Japs," Marines told each other. Sixty nautical miles later, they docked off the Maui coast. "Just another practice run," grumbled the Marines.

"Land the landing craft," coxswains signaled the crude little Higgins boats. The vessels, which had hinged ramps on one end, held 36 men. They bobbed in the surf like pingpong balls in a washing machine.

Marines buckled on "chamberpot" helmets, shrugged into their packs, and adjusted the padding on the straps. Each pack weighed an average of 84.3 pounds. In addition to the clumsy packs, a Marine carried his bulky weapon, which added more weight. A Browning Automatic Rifle weighed 20 pounds, for instance. If a Marine carried a light machine gun, it weighed 36 pounds; a heavy machine gun was four pounds heavier. One of the machine gun squad carried the tripod needed to aim the machine gun, which weighed 53 pounds.

Their packs gave them the shape of a humpback. Worse, when they struggled down the cargo nets into the boats, the packs made them as awkward as turtles. It was risky business. As they dangled on the ropes, some of them lost their footing and swung like Tarzan on a jungle vine. If a man lost his grip, he could fall between his ship and the Higgins boat. In the rough seas, he could easily be crushed between the two. Or his heavy pack could pull him straight to the bottom of the bay.

The goal was to drop or jump into the hull; the trick was to time the leap to land at the crest of the up-and-down bob. Misjudge and even the most skillful coxswain couldn't help you. The lucky Marine made it into the Higgins boat. The unlucky one might be walloped or knocked unconscious or crippled. Maybe even killed.

With everybody finally aboard, the coxswains piloted their boats into rings—one ring for each shorebound wave. First, second, third, and so on. Each craft circled until they received the signal to head in. Then the boats in the first wave fanned out in a broad, single line and roared toward Kahoolawe Island. Jack's boat got the go ahead to join the second wave. They sped the two miles to shore, jockeying through the waves as if they were riding a rollercoaster. Seasick Marines crouched under gunwales and tried to keep from throwing up. Only a few were successful.

Destroyers lobbed shells over their heads, and planes

dive-bombed the beach. Jack's boat crunched on sand. The ramp dropped, and he ran down it and waded ashore. Jack milled around until all the boats raced in. Finally, the regiments established their beachhead along 2,000 yards of shoreline. Jack and his squad set up radios and telephone lines. The message center was open for business.

That night, Jack camped on the side of Maui's volcano, Haleakala. Under orders not to build a fire, he shivered in the cold.

The next morning, Jack and his men reboarded a Higgins boat and rode back out to LST 756. They climbed the net. Then they climbed back down into the landing craft. They repeated the exercise over and over again.

The same exercises went on all the next day, a Sunday. And again the next, a Monday. The troops spent that night on the beach at Lahaina Roads. On Tuesday, they went back out to the LST and started the maneuvers all over again. By then, Jack's back and legs and arms burned like fire. Never before, not even during the most brutal football workouts, had he ever felt so sore and tired.

That afternoon, as the troops flopped on their decks, flagmen started to send semaphore signals between ships. The time had come to sort out the Marines for the long trip to the battle zone. Again, they climbed down the nets and dropped into the flimsy little Higgins boats. The boats transferred the Marines to the ships they would live on during the next several weeks. Jack and his men wound up among the 1,000 troops on the USS *Highlands*.

After the transfers were completed, the ships headed

back to Oahu. That night, January 26, 1945, Jack rode the liberty boat to the Honolulu docks. He attended a farewell luau, or pig roast, honoring high-ranking naval officers and all officers of the Fourth and Fifth divisions. Hostesses were about 70 nurses and Red Cross workers stationed in the Hawaiian Islands. Enlisted men were restricted to their ships.

Juice from roasting beef sizzled as it dripped onto hot rocks. Pigs wrapped in banana leaves were spitted above low fires that had been smoldering in a long ditch all afternoon. The smoky aromas of roasting meat and scorched banana leaves drifted over the grounds.

Native waiters crossed the grounds offering platters of rock crab and gourds filled with Hawaiian stew. They passed around appetizers that included poi, kukui nuts, and local fish. Baskets held such exotic fruits as papaya, pineapple, and peeled raw cane.

Musicians played the islanders' ancient songs on nose-flutes; drummers beat small tom-toms with their knees and elbows. They stomped the rhythms on the ground with their hands or bare feet.

Male and female hula dancers, gardenias perched behind their ears, swayed as ukulele players strummed "Sweet Leilani" and "Lovely Hula Hands." They twitched and stamped with frenzy to the savage "Hawaiian War Chant."

Before the night ended, Jack had drunk some of the potent punch. On his last night ashore, on the eve of battle, he probably drank a *mai tai*, a sweet concoction of rum and pineapple juice. Maybe he drank enough to express some of the fearful thoughts that he normally controlled so well. Maybe he kissed the pretty Red Cross girls. Maybe he forgot where he was headed.

The party ended. Jack stood on the dock in the wee hours of the morning, waiting for a packet boat. His berth was floating somewhere out there in the bay. He helped his friends bellow the songs they had been singing all evening. They sang the sentimental ballads that reminded them of home, of girls, of wives. Then they sang the college fight songs that reminded them of buddies, of football games, of the good old days. They wailed any song that one of them, at least, knew all the words to. And Jack would have sung half a dozen choruses of "Deep in the Heart of Texas."

Late as it was, the parties continued aboard the ships until dawn. Then just as the officers dozed off, the sailors clanged up anchors. The working men of the ships shouted instructions to one another. They brought the ships to life.

The semicircle of the rising sun had just cleared the eastern horizon as the USS *Highlands* nosed out of Pearl Harbor. The ship went through the channel and through the submarine nets.

Joining 21 large troop carriers and their escort of six destroyers, the *Highlands* slipped easily into the zigzag pattern. Bringing up the rear of the convoy was the USS *New York* on its way to bombard an island called Iwo Jima.

The date on the calendar in the deckhouse was

January 27, 1945. Time for the Fourth and Fifth divisions to shove off for a battle three weeks and 5,000 nautical miles away. Time to visit an island where the inhabitants would not crowd the shoreline screaming words of exuberant welcome. Where the missiles they threw would not be coconuts and fruit. The time had come for the boys of the Fifth Division—the Spearhead Division—to strut their stuff. Time for these young Marines, tested and untested, to demonstrate how well they had learned the art of war. Time for Jack and Bill McCann and Wayne Dust to stash their footballs and baseball bats and strut their stuff on another field. On a battlefield.

Jack would have leaned on the rail at the bow of the *Highlands*, his gray-green eyes looking deep and long at the eastern sky. That sky covered his folks, his girl, the Polo Grounds, the bluebonnets of Texas. Everyone and everything he loved.

Behind the ship loomed Diamond Head. Its prow-like visage dimmed and then faded into oblivion. Finally, all he could see was a full moon. Ahead was uncertainty, danger, death... the eternal question of survival.

CHAPTER EIGHTEEN

ISLAND-HOPPING MARINES

Transporting two Marine divisions, their support troops and equipment nearly 5,000 miles was like relocating the entire population of a mid-sized city. It wasn't only that 50,000 Marines had to be moved. They brought along their restaurants, dry goods stores, gunsmith shops, post offices, water works, police department, and sewer system.

What the Marines didn't bring along was a town crier to tell them where they were headed. Then well out to sea, Jack joined the commanding officers on the *Highlands'* top deck. A similar scene was taking place on the other 20 troopships.

The Second Battalion's executive officer brought out a large aerial map and pinned it to the bulkhead. He turned and said, "We will attack an island called Iwo Jima."

Sliding a pointer along intricate charts, the officer

explained that Iwo Jima was a mere splotch in the vast Pacific Ocean. It was so small that a ship might sail past without noticing.

Eleven hundred Japanese civilians inhabited Iwo, along with a few wading birds and thousands of waiting Japanese soldiers. These Japanese were not the ugly, short, bowlegged stereotypes portrayed in Hollywood films. Their commander, Lt. Gen. Tadamichi Kuribayashi, stood five feet nine. As Japan's deputy military attaché, he had spent two years in Washington, D.C. He had studied cavalry tactics at Fort Bliss, traveled around the country, and admired Americans.

The general's tank commander, Lt. Col. Takeichi Nishi, came from a wealthy, old Japanese family. During the 1932 Olympics in Los Angeles, Colonel Nishi and his horse had taken a gold medal in the jumping event.

Nor was Iwo Jima the typical jungle island. Roughly five and a half miles long, two and a half wide, the pork-chop-shaped island contained eight square miles. Navy frogmen had surveyed the island and found that it was volcanic rock, buffeted and scoured by wind and water. The sand on its beaches consisted of calf-deep, gray-black volcanic pumice. It was finer than sand, more the consistency of coarse flour.

Iwo had a desolate terrain. The only vegetation was sparse and scraggly. It was mostly stunted, twisted trees and knife-sharp kunai grass covered with typhus-carrying mites. The island boasted fewer than 10 water wells. Additional water shipped in by tankers was stored in cisterns. Rainwater was collected in barrels and bottles.

On the island's southern tip was the 556-foot-high Mount Suribachi, an inactive volcano. Two miles north of Suribachi stretched a wasteland of humpbacked hills. The hills gradually crawled up to rocky cliffs more than 360 feet high. In the center of the island were two airstrips. North of Airstrip #2, the land stairstepped to the Motoyama Plateau where Korean laborers had started to build a third airstrip. Ugly gorges and deep ravines plunged up to the plateau from the east and west coasts. On the north coast, a jumble of jagged cliffs and ridges looked out across the Pacific Ocean.

The name Iwo Jima translates into English as Sulfur Island. It was an apt name. Jets of green and yellow sulfuric mist escaped from the island's gray-black silt surface. Iwo Jima stank like rotten eggs; the Marines soon dubbed it "the stinking porkchop."

Iwo was important to the Japanese because it guarded the entrance to Tokyo Bay. Part of a chain of islands 660 miles south of Tokyo, Iwo was one of the city's political subdivisions.

Iwo was important to America not simply because of its airfields. It would be the stepping stone for the invasion of Japan proper.

Pilots had been flying over Iwo, snapping photographs. They estimated that the island held 13,000 enemy troops. They later upgraded that figure to 21,000. There actually were 23,000.

General Kuribayashi had positioned hundreds of guns

to fire on almost every square yard of Iwo. To repel landings, he had placed weapons along the coast and had seeded mines along the beaches. He had concealed artillery and antiaircraft weapons in bunkers with steel walls five feet thick. He had hidden rocket launchers in caves and pits. Machine gunners and snipers filled every pillbox. The general had booby-trapped and mined ditches and trenches that Marines might jump into for protection. He had buried heavier mines and dug antitank ditches along routes that American tanks might travel.

Early in the assault, Japanese snipers and artillerymen would fire from the rocky cliffs just north of the west beach. If that didn't stop the Marines, the Japanese would fire heavy artillery and mortar from the center and north sectors of the island.

But first, the Marines would have to get that far. Frogmen indicated that the best landing beach was on Iwo's east coast. It was a strip of black sand six feet wide and two miles long. Then a series of 10 sand terraces ran 600 yards inland. These terraces ranged from eight to 20 feet in height and angled upward at 60 or 70 degrees.

The Marines, wearing 50-pound packs and wading through ankle-deep sand, would find the terraces almost impossible to climb. They would be in full sight of snipers on Suribachi and artillery around Airfield #2.

After their briefing, officers took turns informing the troops of the situation. Jack stood on a hatch and pointed out details on the charts and maps and plaster relief model.

Snapshot taken on Iwo Jima by Ph/M.W.E. Wallace. The exhausted trio in the foreground have been identified as (left to right) 2nd Lt. F.A. Kellogg, W.W. McNaughton, and Jack Lummus. The black lines on the print were apparently caused by concussions from heavy shelling that jarred the film before it was developed. (Photo by PhM 2d Class W.E. Wallace, courtesy Harold L. Pedersen)

Studying the mockups, Jack Carns suddenly recognized what he had guessed two months earlier. The photo in the Honolulu newspaper had shown a Navy plane bombing Iwo Jima. Iwo Jima *was* "Island X." Carns understood, then, why his unit always turned right. The Twenty-seventh would land on the east coast, cross the narrow southern neck of the island, and turn north, up the west coast. *Turn right.*

With every passing day, the convoy sailed farther from Honolulu and closer to Iwo. Jack's nerves tightened like a corkscrew. Yet now that he knew the destination, he felt a sense of purpose. The men, too, seemed more at ease. They played fewer pranks, got into fewer arguments. Men from all backgrounds, from high school dropouts to law students, suddenly shared camaraderie. *We're in this together. You guard my back, and I'll guard yours.* That's what they had learned in boot camp. That's what would get them through the tough times ahead.

To distract attention from the battle to come, musicians played concerts and the troops put on amateur shows. But in the dark of a hot night, quiet reigned in the enlisted men's quarters below. Then might come a mournful whistle, slow and sad: *"My momma done tol' me/when I was in knee pants, son."*

Three days after their briefings, half an hour before midnight, 1,500 miles out of Honolulu, the convoy crossed the 180th meridian, the international date line. Jack "lost" 24 hours of his life. He "lost" Thursday as the date changed from Wednesday, January 31, 1945, to Friday, February 2.

The Navy's crew didn't broadcast the information that an enemy submarine had been trailing them for the past few days. Or that the beautiful full moon made them a brighter target for torpedoes.

Jack wrote home: "Am at sea, headed for combat. Don't worry if I can't write for a while. I'll be okay." He didn't write me. Since the first of the year, I had been writing him every other day. But he hadn't received any mail since he left Camp Tarawa.

On the morning of February 5, Jack sighted Eniwetok, an island Americans had seized from Japan a year before. The *Highlands* entered an immense lagoon and dropped anchor amid a fleet of 250 ships.

Eniwetok didn't resemble the exotic tropical isles of the movies. The island rose only about 10 feet above high tide. Burnt shells of jeeps and tanks, left over from the battle for Eniwetok, littered its tan beaches. Inland, there had once been a lush jungle. Now there were only charred stumps of bombed palm trees and screw pines.

That afternoon, Jack went over the side and swam in the bay's milky waters. Then he went ashore and sat on a screened porch at the two-story officers' club, known all over the Pacific for its long, elaborate bar.

That night, under a potbellied moon, sailors and Marines sat on benches at half a dozen outdoor theaters scattered around the island. Before the movies started, though, a khaki-clad naval officer stepped before the screen and read the latest communique: In the Philippines, 3,500 miles west, General MacArthur's troops had entered Manila. The Army was fighting house-to-house for control of the capital city.

When the armada steamed out of the lagoon at noon the next day, most of the ships went with them. As far as the eye could see, the Pacific Ocean was blanketed by 500 ships. Despite the huge number of ships, enemy submarines surrounded the convoy. Every night, destroyers dropped depth charges.

On February 11, the *Highlands* anchored eight miles out in the sapphire waters of Saipan's harbor. Seven months earlier, the Second and Fourth Marine divisions, with the Army's Twenty-seventh Infantry, had fought a fierce battle for the island. Jack wanted to go ashore and visit Jack Casey's grave in the Marine cemetery. But no liberties were granted.

Late that afternoon, a deafening roar erupted from the southern tip of the island. Every 45 seconds, one of the Twentieth Air Force's B-29 bombers lifted off Aslito Air Base's airstrip. The huge, silver Superfortresses weighed 70 tons when fully loaded with gas and bombs. When they gained altitude, the planes swung north, headed for their nightly bombing run on Tokyo. The round trip totaled 3,200 miles.

The next day, Valentine's Day, Vice Adm. Richmond Turner held a press conference for 70 war correspondents. Turner, commander of all forces involved with the Iwo invasion, informed the press he would personally censor all their dispatches coming out of Iwo Jima.

Admiral Turner didn't discuss the argument that had broken out between Marine and Navy commanders. The Marines had requested a concentrated seven-day bombardment before the invasion started. However, the Navy had sent most of its big guns to Okinawa for a pre-invasion bombardment there. The Navy hoped to blunt the Marines' anger with three days of shelling.

Even so, Admiral Turner predicted that invasion-day casualties might rise as high as 40 percent. "Many men who love life are about to die," he said, startling combat-hardened war correspondents.

While the reporters quizzed the admiral, the Navy transferred all Marines who would be in the first 10 waves to LSTs. Jack, who would go ashore in the second wave, boarded LST 756 again. With amphibious tractors in the holds and troops sharing the decks with jeeps, the LSTs steamed away from Saipan. Three miles southwest, they dropped anchor off the Tinian coast. There, with planes soaring overhead, they conducted another rehearsal. When the seas turned rough, several Marines were injured.

The next day, the bouncing LSTs brought their boat-loads of seasick Marines back to Saipan Harbor. Medics dusted the Marines with DDT. "Now we can kill a mosquito just by spitting on it," griped a Marine.

Jack noticed that the ships slated to bombard Iwo Jima had already left. Carriers bound for an air strike against Tokyo had also gone.

At dusk that evening, Jack's LST steamed out of Saipan Harbor. It joined the convoy heading northwest to Iwo Jima. They had 700 miles to go and three days to get there.

This was the real McCoy. No more dress rehearsals.

The next day, the rest of the Fourth and Fifth divisions sailed out of the harbor. With them was the Third Marine Division, which had come from Guam. The line of 800 ships heading for Iwo Jima was 75 miles long.

Jack quickly realized that an LST offered few comforts.

An awkward vessel, the ship wallowed and careened through the ocean at five to seven knots. It resembled a tipsy, 300-foot-long wooden shoe. The shallow-draft LST had been designed to haul amphibious tanks and landing craft, along with a crew of 98 sailors. Nearly every LST headed for Iwo also carried 217 Marines.

The ship provided bunks for only 70. The Marines, then, spent 24 hours a day on open deck. Tanks and jeeps that wouldn't fit in the hold took up most of the deck space. A landing craft swung from a davit next to the radio shack; ammunition occupied the tail of the ship; and drums of 80-octane gas sloshed on the starboard side. Packs leaned every which way, and drying laundry pinned to haphazard lines snapped in the wind.

Jammed on top of each other, the Marines slept in any spot they found. Poncho-covered cots lined available deck space, leaving just enough room at the ends for a man to sidle through. There weren't enough cots to go around, and a few boys discovered mattresses in the deckhouse. Others claimed the stack of life rafts or crawled into gun mounts. But most curled on rusted deck plates, using lifejackets for pillows.

Mostly, the food consisted of soggy C rations washed down with powdered lemonade that one Marine complained tasted like sheep urine. Nothing tasted good. Gas coming out of the LST's smokestack coated everything, even their tongues, with an oily film. Crates of wilting cabbages sat on the deck, adding another bad odor. Refuse and clutter resisted frequent attempts to swab down the decks.

The men attended briefings. They stood guard. They took gun watches. Four hours on, eight off. Officers took naps in a fan-cooled cabin or swapped stories of beautiful women they'd known back in the States. They tried to act nonchalant but were just as worried as the enlisted men.

Jack spent most of his time on deck, joking with the men. He used every method he knew to ease their fears. At daily church services, he stood tall and tan and lean, head bowed, clutching his baseball cap.

A destroyer drew alongside LST 756 and dropped off a mail sack. The men crowded around the mail clerk until they learned that the sack contained letters for the Eighth Marine Regiment.

Their second day out of Saipan, Jack stood in the radio shack listening to reports of the bombardment. Rear Admiral W. H. P. Blandy's fleet of six battleships and five cruisers circled Iwo, lobbing bombs and catapulting spotter planes off their decks. The pilots, complaining about thick black smoke from antiaircraft fire, radioed back directions for first one target, then another.

Then it began to rain, and the planes returned to their carriers. Thick clouds also turned 42 B-24 bombers back to the Marianas. The rain became a heavy downpour, and Admiral Blandy cancelled the bombardment.

Jack attended a wardroom briefing. His heart sank as the intelligence officer passed on information about Iwo's massive defense fortifications. The more Jack heard, the darker the picture looked. What about "five days, maybe ten?" he asked himself. What about "two weeks at the most?"

"No use kidding ourselves," said an operations officer. "We've got the biggest fleet in history with us, but this is going to be a tough one."

On February 18, LST 756 arrived eight miles off Iwo Jima. Jack couldn't see the island. He saw red and white flashes as the ships lobbed their 14-inch shells.

The ship bustled as everyone got ready to leave. Officers issued ammunition, Japanese yen, and a two-day supply of canned rations. The men stripped their packs of anything they wouldn't need in combat. They carried spoons, cigarettes in tin cans, salt tablets, and razors. Jack found room for the palm-sized New Testament he'd received from the California evangelist, Aimee Semple McPherson.

Carrying his carbine, he waddled into the mess compartment. Hooked to his web belt were his canteen, a Kabar knife, first-aid kit, mess kit, and grenades. Strapped to his backpack were his shelter half and poncho. Across his chest was an extra bandoleer of ammunition. He ate a heaping plate of ham steak, potatoes, and green beans. After C rations, it tasted like manna from Heaven.

After supper, Jack went to the galley and joined 100 Protestants for communion. On the deck, another hundred Catholics heard the priest celebrate Mass.

Soon the sun went down. The darkening sky made it easier to pinpoint Iwo Jima. It sparkled with red explosions of Navy rockets. Jack heard the "thump," "bump," "thud" of detonations. He saw a huge white flash.

A crowd of Marines huddled around a shortwave radio. Jack went over and heard the end of a Benny Goodman record. Then he heard Tokyo Rose's voice, speaking Americanized English. Broadcasting from Tokyo, she taunted the Marines. She knew they were on their way to Iwo Jima after stops at Eniwetok and Saipan. She identified the various units poised to invade Iwo. She listed the vessels around their LST and told how many Marines were on board each ship.

"It doesn't matter how tough other landings have been," she warned, "they were easy as pie. Wait until you see the surprises our lionhearted General Kuribayashi and his valiant warriors have in store for you."

One of the boys looked around him fearfully. Jack calmed him down by explaining that Tokyo Rose got her information from the crew of the submarine that had been trailing them.

Jack walked into the wardroom. Shadows flickered on the big maps pinned to the bulkhead. A couple of lieutenants played cards, slapping their discards down on the green tablecloth. Two others hunched over a chessboard.

Jack deciphered a message coming in from the command ship. It outlined the situation:

Heavy clouds forced the B-24s to cease bombing that day. However, the "Ugly Ducklings" had already bombed Iwo for 74 consecutive days. During the past three days, six battleships and five cruisers had fired 14,000 rounds at Sulfur Island. The shelling had demolished or damaged most strongholds on the east beach. However, they had hit only half of 200 targets. They hadn't made a dent in the underground bunkers Kuribayashi had installed inland.

Even after such a dismal assessment, the commanders decided not to delay the invasion. As planned, the Marines would go ashore at nine the next morning, February 19.

Jack realized that the invasion would be especially tough on the Fifth Division Marines. Forty percent were battle-hardened Raiders and Paratroopers. The rest had never faced an enemy, never fought a battle. The Fourth Division, on the other hand, would invade its fourth island in 13 months. The Third Division, veterans of the Bougainville and Guam campaigns, would remain aboard their ships for the first few days.

Jack's Twenty-seventh Regiment was to land on Red Beach One and push across the island's narrow neck to the west beach. Then they were to head north and secure the first airfield. To the Twenty-seventh's left, the Twenty-eighth Regiment would go in on Green Beach. Their mission was to scale Mount Suribachi, digging the enemy from caves and bunkers. To the Twenty-seventh's right, the Fourth Division's Twenty-third Regiment would head up Iwo's east coast and take the high ground between the two airfields. When the Americans controlled Suribachi and occupied the first airfield, the Third Division would come ashore. They were to go up the center of the island.

Yes, it was a big job. Jack figured it could go quickly or it could fail miserably. Feeling uneasy, he left the wardroom and picked his way among the Marines. Fully dressed, they sprawled all over the deck. Some wrote letters, others sharpened bayonets or blackened the sights of their rifles and carbines. A BAR man checked to see if he had enough clips for his Browning Automatic Rifle; a crew of machine gunners checked their ammunition belts. Boys rummaged in their packs, checking their rations, shaving gear, skivvies, clean socks, snapshots of the folks.

It was quiet. Jack heard the LST's engines throb as they idled in forward, then reverse, maintaining their position in the fleet. A boy jumped up and ran for the head, holding his stomach. He could blame it on the ship's jerky roll.

It was nighttime. Time to sleep. But who could sleep? Someone started to tell a joke then forgot the punch line. Someone else wanted to laugh, but nothing seemed quite as funny as it had a day or so before.

Pfc. Don Hamilton stood at the rail. He stared through the cold darkness at the faint flashes. The distant rumble made him jumpy. He reminded himself that he could only die once. Maybe he'd be lucky and get one of those million-dollar wounds the guys talked about. Not bad enough to kill or maim him. But bad enough that he could go home to Indiana and see his wife and babies.

Jack also leaned on the rail, listening to the sinister rumble coming from the island. An icy chill swept over him. He felt apprehensive, the same as he always did in those jittery moments before a big game. Tomorrow, though, it would be him against the bullets and missiles of an enemy who hated him. Sweat popped out on his forehead, made clammy by the night breeze. His knees shook. Would they shake when he waded through the surf in a few hours? he wondered. Would they shake when he ran messages the next day? As the battalion's liaison officer, he would be its trouble shooter between the Second Battalion command post, the regiment, and the other units around them.

Jack looked around him, at the boys waiting for dawn. He thought of the year he'd spent with the 200 Marines of Fox Company. He hoped he'd taught them what they would need to live through the next days. Please, God, he prayed, let them use it well.

CHAPTER NINETEEN

THE INVASION

At three hours past midnight, the loudspeaker crackled. "Now hear this, now hear this. Marines fall in. Full combat gear." The date was Monday, February 19, 1945.

If the announcement woke anyone up, it didn't wake Jack Lummus. He had been sitting on a hatch, counting stars. The sky was so dark and the stars so brilliant, it looked as if the angels had been up all night, scattering diamonds.

After a struggle, Jack managed to fit his pack over his combat jacket. He picked up his carbine and went to ask the first mate about the weather. The temperature was 68 degrees. There was a light north breeze and a calm sea.

A large force of battlewagons had moved to within three miles of Iwo Jima's east beach. At 0330, they began a five-hour bombardment. Jack saw tiny yellow flashes and heard the distant rumble of gunfire. Then tracers arced through the sky, showing sailors the bearings of the big cannon shells they were firing. The LST had moved closer by then, and when the shells exploded on land now, Jack saw flashes of pink and purple and orange. An occasional gray-black mushroom cloud arose when a shell struck an oil dump.

"Now hear this, now hear this," the voice on the loud-speaker clattered at 0445. "You'll have tenderloin steak sandwiches for breakfast. This will be your last meal before debarking." And then a hesitant "Good luck!"

Two hundred Marines stacked helmets and weapons on top of their backpacks and lined up for the last hot meal they would eat in a long, long time. For some, it would be the last meal, period.

"Now hear this, now hear this," came the clatter again. "All Marines below to the tank deck. Man your debarka-tion stations."

Marines, their faces smeared with black camouflage grease, snaked into the hold. Amtracs and an assortment of other landing vehicles already jammed the hold. The closed area rang with excited shouts.

A chaplain crawled into a landing craft. His lips moved, but the high-pitched whine of starting engines and cherry-bomb backfires drowned out his words. As coxswains revved up their engines, blue smoke and car-bon monoxide snorted out of exhaust pipes. The vehicles lined up, side by side, their steel cleats scraping and clat-tering on the rough deck. They rattled like the links of a

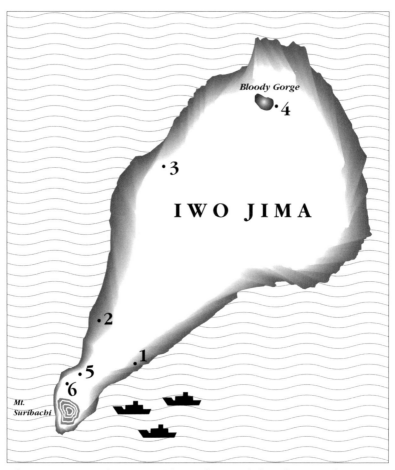

The Marines named Iwo Jima "The Stinking Porkchop" because of its chop-like shape and because of the unpleasant sulfurous smell.

1. *A few minutes past nine on the morning of February 19, Jack landed with the Fifth Division's Twenty-seventh Regiment Second Battalion on Red Beach One.*
2. *By nightfall Jack's unit was fighting across the neck of the island.*
3. *For the next 16 days, the Fifth Division struggled northward against fiercely desperate Japanese troops.*
4. *At a rough, strategic ravine called the "Gorge," Jack Lummus took command of Company E's Third platoon.*
5. *Lummus is carried back to the hospital tent.*
6. *Jack Lummus is buried under a plain white cross in the military cemetery*

thousand chains.

An officer held a megaphone and yelled boat numbers through it. Another officer called roll from a crumpled roster sheet. "Second Battalion headquarters, stand by to disembark," the officer hollered. "Communications platoon stand by to disembark." That was Jack's signal. In the dark, he and 40 others bumped into each other as they boarded their amtrac.

No turning back now. Pack straps chafed necks. Breathing became ragged. Faces looked pinched and white. Almost everyone became uncomfortably aware of bladders and wished they had gone to the head again. A rifle clanged against another's helmet. Under *his* helmet, Jack wore his lucky Baylor baseball cap.

By 0630, half the Marines on LST 756 stood in amtracs, waiting to leave.

"Execute! Speed zero." Two doors, 15 feet high, grated open. Dim daylight burst in. Dawn had come. A ramp ground down. The LST's hold throbbed with the roar of motors. The lead amtrac jerked forward and tilted down the ramp. It dropped into the water, out of sight. One by one, the assault boats splashed into the ocean.

"Yahoo! Yahoo!" someone yelled.

The amtrac carrying Jack belched forward. It crossed the ramp and teetered for a long moment on the edge. Then it plunged into the ocean. Jack's stomach lurched, and his feet fell out from under him. Water cans and ammunition cases barked his shins. This is like riding a rollercoaster, he thought.

Rolling and bucking, its colorful flags snapping in the breeze, the vehicle skidded away from the LST. Jack felt as if he was riding the ocean's swells in his mother's galvanized wash tub.

Blue-shirted sailors lined the LST's rail. They cheered and made the V for Victory sign. "Happy D-Day to you, happy D-Day to you," someone sang.

The amtrac seemed to be aiming for the huge fleet of cruisers and battleships that had moved in during the night. The ships were lobbing shells at Iwo, point-blank. Jack's vehicle chugged past a battleship's steel-gray, skyscraper sides. More sailors waved coffee cups and formed a V with their fingers. The ship's fire rings ground out. With an earsplitting "boom," a salvo whanged overhead and disappeared in the direction of the island. The concussion's recoil made the huge ship roll. Its wake nearly swamped the amtrac.

The amtrac lurched on. "All right, you people, time to hunker down," ordered the coxswain.

At 0730, the bombardment ceased and B-24 Liberators flew in. One by one, they dropped out of formation and made passes over the island. Missiles fell out of bomb bays. They exploded and huge pillars of smoke rose.

The amtrac reached its assembly area, two miles offshore. A control vessel met them and took them to their boat lane. The amtrac glided into a ring of 500 idling boats that were slowly circling a mother ship.

The B-24s left and the battleships resumed shelling. After 35 minutes, the barrage stopped again. Seventy-two dive bombers and fighter planes appeared. They showered Mount Suribachi with rockets and bombs and strafed its slopes with machine gun fire. Flying low, the planes dumped napalm over the rugged high ground to the north. Americans didn't start using napalm until 1942. It is a jellied incendiary petroleum compound that bursts into violent plumes of flame.

At 0815, a signalman on the central control vessel snapped his signal flags. Sixty-eight landing craft of the first wave pulled out of the circle. They plowed to the destroyer stationed at the point of departure. The amtracs and landing boats formed a line two miles long.

With the first wave in place, the signalman snapped his flags again. The diesel engine of Jack's amtrac roared, and the boat surged out of the circle. They jockeyed into formation 250 yards behind the first wave. Seventy amtracs carrying Jack Lummus and 1,360 other Marines made up the second wave. Then, 250 yards behind Jack's amtrac, the third wave took up its position. Behind them, the other seven waves formed.

At exactly 0830, the planes disappeared, and the control vessel dropped signal flags from the yardarm. The signal meant: "Execute first wave."

The first string of amtracs crossed the imaginary line of departure. They bore south toward the destroyers and rocket ships waiting to lead the waves in. Sailing abreast, the ships laid down a phosphorous smoke screen and lobbed 40mm missiles at the beach. Their shells exploded 200 feet aboveground and raked the island with hot-steel shrapnel. An enemy shell blasted a hole in a landing craft. Water spurted from its side. Meanwhile, the battleships continued to fire their big shells onto the high ground of Iwo's central ridges. A destroyer ahead of the first wave lobbed five-inch shells low onto the beach. Dust, debris, and chunks of earth spun drunkenly in midair until they sank back to disappear in the rolling smoke.

Five minutes after the first wave started for shore, the second wave's control boat fired a red flare. Red for Red Beach one. "Here we go," Jack shouted. "Let's do it right."

Jack's amtrac headed for the minesweeper that would escort the second wave in. An ensign stood on the minesweeper's deck. "Boat, ahoy," he hailed. A Marine lieutenant in the lead attack boat raised his bullhorn. "Ready to proceed to point of departure."

"Follow us," the ensign responded.

Spray drenched Jack as the amtrac churned 50 yards behind the minesweeper. Bobbing like corks, the amtracs in the second wave switched to a zigzag pattern to evade the increasing fire coming from Suribachi and the cliffs to the north.

As the amtrac sped closer to shore, Jack could hear that the thunder of bombardment was growing in intensity. But all he could see were the sheer rock cliffs and the smoky peak of Suribachi. The red fires of explosions dotted Iwo's central spine. Towers of soot billowed skyward.

The ships leading the first wave separated and peeled off to the left and right. The first wave wallowed on toward the deafening roar. Five minutes to shore. A flight of Corsairs zoomed in from the south. Flying low, they laid strings of bombs along the shoreline and strafed Suribachi with .50-caliber bullets.

Enemy antiaircraft fire caught a Navy Hellcat fighter plane. The plane flared as it plummeted into the ocean. A two-man observation plane flying above Suribachi burst into flames. It looped on its back and crashed between two amtracs.

Then the planes left, and the Navy started firing again. The minesweeper heeled to starboard and circled around behind the second wave. The amtracs and landing craft bobbed alone. The frail vessels bounced and reeled toward shore.

A fusillade battered the side of the boat. Everyone ducked. The first wave landed. Jack could see Marines scrambling up the sandy dunes. He glanced at his wristwatch. The time was 0859. His amtrac neared the shoreline. A great plume of sand and seawater towered on their right. Machine gun and rifle bullets slammed against the armor.

The skipper cut the engine. Rough surf rocked their boat like a cradle. They inched forward.

The platoon sergeant ran along the narrow gunwale to the ramp. He stood on the grating beside the pilot.

"Lock and load," he roared. "Now lock and load." Over his shoulder, the sergeant watched the coxswain. His hand gripped the ramp catch. His face, shadowed by his helmet, looked strange, as if chiseled out of marble.

A geyser skyrocketed on the left. Suddenly, the amtrac smoothed out like a Cadillac. Then the boat's hull scraped on the bottom with a violent jerk, a grinding, lifting jolt. The coxswain clashed gears. The boat shuddered and waddled forward on its treads like a crippled turtle. It swung to an angle and stopped dead. Men sprawled over each other, wild-eyed, clutching and cursing.

"Stand by," the sergeant yelled. The amtrac bogged down at the shoreline. The coxswain gestured at the sergeant. "Let the ramp down," he said. The sergeant released the catch and shouted something. Jack couldn't understand the words, and somehow it seemed a matter of life and death that he do so.

The ramp slammed down into ankle-deep surf. "Wire," someone shouted. "Watch out for wire."

Jack rolled over the back of the amtrac, the seaward side. He came around to the front in the shallow water and ran up on the sandy beach, rifle high and ready. But "running" was impossible. He sank to his ankles in the bottomless black ash.

It was urgent to find cover. Six feet inland, Jack ran up against the first sandy terrace. It was 10 to 15 feet high. Floundering in the sand, he struggled to climb the steep incline. Some of the men around him flopped to the ground on their stomachs, clawing the sand, trying to "swim" through it. Others crawled on hands and knees. Still others tried to dig down to solid rock.

Incoming troops stumbled across bodies. Some of the bodies were dead Marines waiting to be covered with ponchos. But most were alive, boys waiting for orders, waiting to see someone from their unit, waiting to be told what to do.

By 0900, Maj. John Antonelli, Jack's commanding officer, had landed on Red Beach One and was setting up Second Battalion headquarters. Right behind Major Antonelli came the staff of Col. Thomas A. Wornham's Twenty-seventh regimental headquarters.

As each unit landed, it fired an amber parachute flare to signal its arrival to the colonel, who watched through powerful binoculars from the control ship out at sea. The fifth flare went up at exactly 0906.

It would be two days before telephone wires would be strung between the two headquarters, and radios still weren't set up. So Jack Lummus started running—literally running—to relay messages between Antonelli and other commanders.

Commanding officers of companies and battalions on the move passed orders by way of arm and hand signals. Or if the units weren't in eye contact, the commander yelled an order and a runner took off with the message.

By 0911, however, regimental headquarters did have radios, and Colonel Wornham radioed the USS *Eldorado*: "Landings on schedule. Casualties unexpectedly light. Proceeding toward airstrip against light resistance."

At first the resistance *was* light. General Kuribayashi had expected the Marines to come in on the west beach. It took a few minutes to turn his guns around.

Major Antonelli ordered Easy and Fox companies over

the dunes. Within 20 minutes, wide lines of rifle companies had conquered the terraces and had started to plod inland.

When they scaled the last terrace, the Marines became confused. The Navy's shelling had destroyed most landmarks, and the troops couldn't orient themselves. They blundered ahead, praying they were going in the right direction.

Meanwhile, Easy Company advanced 50 yards. The Marines formed squads and platoons and started across an open plateau. They wound through scrawny trees and into a network of recently vacated trenches and antitank ditches. Then Easy ran into its first pillbox. Rifle and machine gun bullets spewed from a black hole, and Marines lunged into craters and depressions. A runner raced to the beach and came back with a team of flamethrowers. Jets of burning gasoline soon cleared the way. By then, Easy Company had suffered its first casualty.

One hundred yards ahead, Fox Company ran into a trench with 20 Japanese in it. The platoon took cover until a team of machine gunners arrived.

Back on the beach, the situation worsened. At 1000, the enemy got its guns turned around. Mortar and small-arms fire rained down on 6,000 Marines. Many got caught out in the open along the strip of sand. The Twenty-eighth Regiment was a long way from conquering the snipers on Mount Suribachi; the Fourth Marine Division was having a struggle to get up on the ridges into the high plateau.

Shouts of "corpsman!" rang out above the thunder of barrage. Wounded Marines toppled next to dead Marines. Medics and chaplains scurried to attend the wounded. A bullet killed one Marine even as a Catholic chaplain comforted him. The priest administered last rites.

Then Capt. Bill McCann, one of Jack's baseball teammates and commanding officer of Company E, was shot in the neck. A corpsman treated him and sent him back to the beach to be evacuated to a hospital ship.

So far, the Navy had brought in the first 10 waves of Marines and high-priority supplies, such as ammunition, radios, medical supplies, rations, and water. Colonel Wornham got on the radio to his shipboard command: "All units pinned down by artillery and mortar fire. Casualties heavy. Need tank support fast to move anywhere." Then the Fourth Division suffered a deluge of enemy shelling. Commanders all up and down the beach joined the Colonel's plea for tanks.

High winds came up and buffeted the island. Amtracs broached in the rough surf, seawater flooded engines, and vehicles drifted helplessly, getting in the way of incoming boats. Disabled and wallowing vessels were hurled onto the beaches, already jammed with bogged-down landing craft, burning jeeps, and dozens of other crippled vehicles.

Not long after Wornham's SOS, ships started unloading the big, olive-green Sherman tanks. Sixteen tanks arrived on Yellow Beach, but three of them struck land mines. Two tanks rolled onto Red Beach. A third fell overboard.

Another 14 tanks finally made it to the beach, only to become stalled in a gigantic traffic jam. For 50 minutes, Japanese antitank weapons pummeled the Shermans.

Then the mighty tanks started to lumber up the first terrace. They slipped and slithered, unable to gain traction in the soft sand until bulldozers roared off landing craft and cut lanes through the dunes. In a single file, the Shermans labored onto the plateau.

Meanwhile, Marines trying to cross the neck of the island ran up against pillboxes. They had been trained to work in teams against the bunkers. Riflemen would fire at the gun port while one of their men ran up and shoved in a package of dynamite, called a satchel charge. Faced with a real situation, however, the Marines discovered that the Japanese didn't wait for the explosion. They fled into their escape tunnels. When the Marines went on, the Japanese came back and fired at the Americans' backs.

The Marines cheered when the first Sherman tank arrived and poured 75mm shells into a pillbox. When Easy Company started forward again, the men moved so fast that they stumbled into Fox Company. Easy and Fox companies gained another 100 yards before enemy spotters zeroed in on their tanks. The Marines found that running beside a tank was a mixed blessing. Tanks made easy targets. Snipers on Suribachi poured fire down on them. They radioed the tanks' positions to Japanese mortarmen on the ridges above the airfield. Soon rocket and mortar shells rained down on the tanks.

Then Easy and Fox companies blundered into a

Japanese antitank ditch that angled across the island. Halting often to scout ahead, they straggled single-file. Between them and their goal were dozens of underground emplacements. Some were pillboxes shaped like igloos or cones; others were bunkers with patches of grass and low shrubs planted on their roofs. From a distance, they looked like harmless rises.

At 1035, three Marines from the Twenty-eighth Regiment reached a cliff overlooking the west beach. A few minutes later, six more Marines pushed through. Within half an hour, another platoon from the Twenty-eighth joined them. Behind this vanguard, ragged lines of the Fifth Division stretched across the neck of Iwo Jima, cutting Suribachi off from the rest of the island.

Easy and Fox companies had tough going, advancing only a few yards at a time. A couple of men would stand up, sprint to the nearest shell crater, and drop into it. Two or three others followed. Sometimes they wormed forward on their hands and knees or scooted on their bottoms into depressions.

The Twenty-seventh Regiment advanced so fast that Jack and his unit couldn't keep up. Not being able to confer with their lines frustrated both Major Antonelli and Colonel Wornham.

The word "line," though, didn't apply to Iwo Jima. The front line wobbled in and out. It reminded Don Hamilton of a prairie dog town. "You looked around and saw no one," Hamilton explained. The Americans were in foxholes. The Japanese were underground in pillboxes and bunkers.

In the early afternoon, Colonel Wornham learned that the First Battalion had reached the edge of the airfield. Then Major Antonelli heard that Easy Company had passed the southwest corner of the airstrip and was on the opposite beach, awaiting orders.

Antonelli took stock: Fox Company had lost half its men. Easy Company had lost its leader, Bill McCann, and fifteen others. Six had been killed, nine wounded.

He sent Jack to regimental headquarters with the message: "Tony is ready to make his turn up the west beach." Jack brought back permission to swing north toward the airfield.

A Fox Company platoon headed for a bluff 200 yards up a road. Shells poured down from ridges and high ground. Every yard cost wounded and dead. But the men pushed on up the hill.

Then the platoon ran into a huge pillbox wedged into the bluff. Five blockhouses surrounding the pillbox pinned the platoon in a fusillade of fire. Easy Company was in trouble, too, and tanks couldn't get through to help. For almost an hour, both companies tried to retreat, but they couldn't move. Finally a sergeant from Fox Company put together an oversized TNT satchel. He slipped up on the pillbox and tossed the packet inside. The explosion killed the occupants.

Fox started ahead again but encountered snipers in a thicket of blasted, shrub-like trees. Fox Company had butted up against a 700-man Japanese infantry battalion.

Dog Company sent a platoon to support Fox. A sergeant led his squad into the thicket and flushed out the snipers that had stymied Fox. The sergeant and one of his men paid for their bravery with their lives.

Back on the east beach, Colonel Wornham called for the Twenty-sixth Regiment to be brought in from the ships. A dangerous situation had developed. The Twenty-seventh had swung north to attack the airfield. The Twenty-eighth Regiment had turned south to assault Mount Suribachi. The maneuver left a big gap between the two regiments. The Twenty-sixth would have to fill the void.

By the time the Twenty-sixth arrived, 30,000 Marines were on Iwo Jima.

Wornham's voice had also been heard on the radio, insisting that artillery be sent in before dark.

As the sun lowered, the landing beach resembled the wreckage after a tornado. Enemy shells had demolished incoming equipment. Debris, flung haphazardly through the air, had injured or killed Marines as they tried to unload supplies and machines. Under the lip of the first terrace, Navy doctors and corpsmen worked in crude first-aid stations.

The beach was so congested that nothing could move onto or away from it. Waiting offshore to unload were DUKWs bringing in howitzers, as well as landing craft with tanks, trucks, and jeeps. Farther out, channels were blocked by boats and heavy equipment that had been hit, burned, broached, capsized, mangled, and otherwise rendered worthless.

Then the heroic captain of LST 779 rammed his bow through the wreckage. The vessel's huge doors creaked open, and its ramp rattled down. Tractors hooked cables onto four 155mm howitzers and pulled them out. They worked the two-and-a-half-ton weapons up terraces and across the island to the Twenty-seventh Marines.

The engineers laid down Marsden matting. Amphibious tractors and tracked Weasels ground up the terraces, carrying supplies directly to the front.

Heavy artillery arrived to bolster the Twenty-eighth Regiment's efforts to scale Suribachi's approaches. The regiment started up, but when the enemy poured gunfire down on them, they fell back. Those Marines needed their tanks, most of which had become stuck on the beach or had been demolished by enemy antitank shells.

Just before dark, some of the Fifth Division's commanders came ashore. Brig. Gen. Leo D. Hermle set up his command post near Airfield #1. Colonel Wornham moved regimental headquarters 200 yards farther west. Major Antonelli moved his battalion headquarters 200 yards ahead of Wornham's. At 1700, General Hermle sent a runner to Wornham. "Button up. Dig in for the night." Jack ran the message to Major Antonelli. Easy, Dog, and Fox companies dug foxholes two feet deep, six feet long.

By the time darkness fell, the Marines had settled in. They were too tired to eat and too numb to remember that it had been more than 12 hours since their last meal. They heard the beginnings of the constant gunfire that would keep them awake all night long. They heard the enemy slap their rifle butts and scream: *"United States Marines be dead tomorrow."*

The Navy started firing parachute flares. All night, the brightness would discourage the Japanese from mounting *banzai* attacks.

Jack Lummus spent the night carrying messages back and forth between command posts, as commanders tallied up their gains and losses. Marines held less than 10 percent of the island. The Fourth occupied the east edge of the airfield, the Fifth the west. The Fourth had lost one-fourth of its troops that first day. Some were killed, some wounded. The Fifth lost 600.

Then almost like a miracle, Supply Sgt. Ray Dooley and his crew showed up, driving an Army DUKW. They made a long sweep behind the front lines and tossed out bundles of ammunition and rations.

Marines appeared. Their dungarees were covered with dirt, their faces streaked with a paste of black sand, their eyes with a vacant thousand-yard stare. Unable to light fires, they filled their bellies with a cold concoction of stew or hash or corned beef and Navy beans. At least it was food.

CHAPTER TWENTY

DRIVING NORTH

At night, between two and four Marines occupied each foxhole. Each man took his turn at guard, four hours on, four off. He could have read a newspaper, so bright was the island lit by yellow flares. As they floated to earth on silk parachutes, the flares faded to green, then snuffed out.

The firing went on all night, as loud and constant as it had been all day. Every 20 seconds, a shell from one of the Navy's guns thundered overhead. It sounded like a flapping window shade. From behind the line of fox-holes, American artillery fired a mortar that "fizzed" as it went by. Enemy spigot mortars wobbled past, screeching. Their explosions shook the earth. Small arms fire chattered, and the guard tensed, straining to see what the guy in the next foxhole was shooting at. The boy's heart pounded at the slightest noises. They all sounded like stealthy footfalls.

Jack Lummus spent his nights at the Second Battalion's command post, which was as busy as a hill of red Texas ants. Temperatures fell when the sun went down, and Jack tugged on his combat jacket. Officers pored over maps then sent Jack running to the command post next door with orders.

The sky lightened, and Marines ventured out of their holes to begin what would be a daily routine. They changed socks, poured an inch of water into their helmets, and rinsed their faces. They choked down cheese-and-cracker rations and cold instant coffee.

Spreading out their ponchos, Marines field-stripped their weapons, brushed off sand and dirt, and ran lead-weighted thongs through the barrels. Then they oiled their carbines and snapped in clips.

At 0740, the fleet returned and resumed shelling. Explosions roared and black smoke boiled up in columns. The Fifth's artillery opened up. "S-s-s-schunk...s-s-s-schunk." Mortarmen "walked" hundreds of shells up and down the terrain ahead. Shrapnel and bullets whined as Japanese fired from cliff faces and Americans fired back. The air stunk of cordite.

Trucks ran over the phone lines Jack's communications unit had finally strung, chewing them to bits. Forward posts relied on radios but ran short of batteries. Jack continued to deliver messages.

On his sprints, Jack saw carrier-based planes dropping bombs on Suribachi. The Navy's big shells and shells from tanks, halftracks, and artillery exploded. The volcano was wreathed in smoke; its interior even rumbled.

Hard to see in the murk, the Twenty-eighth Regiment advanced slowly toward the mountain's base. They stormed hundreds of pillboxes, caves, bunkers, and one-man spider holes with their flame-throwers, grenades, and satchels.

The Twenty-seventh's orders were to secure Motoyama Airfield #1 and overrun the main island defense. Their advance resembled a game of hopscotch. As one unit wore out or bogged down or lost a lot of men, another unit would push through to take up the assault.

Fox Company moved 200 yards, only to be stopped by a deluge of heavy artillery rockets and mortar shells. They met a barrier of pillboxes and spider traps.

By mid-afternoon, Fox pushed through, and the regiment seized the section of Airfield #1 that lay in their zone. To their right, the Fourth Division conquered the airfield's eastern sector. Casualties ran high.

Seabees and Army crews brought in bulldozers and earth movers. Two thousand strong, they worked around the clock and under sniper fire, lengthening the landing strip to 5,000 feet. The generals planned to bring part of the Third Division out of reserves. They needed the runway to launch an assault against Motoyama Airfield #2.

Meanwhile, the Fifth and Fourth advanced to the southern tip of Airfield #2. Its defenders moved to higher ground. The Marines ran into one ridge after another. They called it "The Rockpile." Marines fought up one slope and gained the top. Beyond, there was always another ravine or hill. As Marines swarmed into the ravine, Japanese fired down on them from the top of the next ridge.

At one dark moment, the Second Battalion also received a barrage when the Twenty-sixth Regiment's artillery fired on them accidentally. By the time they corrected their error, 25 Fox Company Marines had been hit.

Jack surveyed the carnage. The dead bodies dotting the sands dismayed him. Nobody died as neatly as they had in the Saturday afternoon cowboy movies of his youth. These were violent deaths. "It's worse than you could ever imagine," he wrote in one of his few letters home.

In the turmoil of battle, word reached troops on the front lines that the Fifth Division's post office was open for business. But the Marines were trying to stay alive. They were too busy to go back and get their mail.

The situation worsened for the Twenty-seventh when they smacked up against General Kuribayashi's heavy cross-island defense. A wide belt of 1,500 caves, bolstered by hundreds of concrete and steel pillboxes, ran across the island. The Fourth Division had been stymied by the huge rampart since the first day.

At dusk that evening, a chill wind brought a slow, steady rain. Cold water drenched Jack's poncho and the legs of his dungarees. It funnelled into the neck of his combat jacket and his boot tops. Volcanic ash mixed with rain plastered his ruddy complexion with a gray paste. When he tried to wipe the raindrops off his carbine, the sand from his hands stuck to the stock. His lips turned blue, and shivers wracked his tall frame.

That night, 800 Japanese massed along the Fifth Division's left flank. They chose that night because rain had snuffed out parachute flares, making the attackers invisible. Rain also hampered Marine artillery fire. Japanese and Americans battled in close-quarter combat. The Japanese turned back, but they returned in a short while. This time they hid in wrecked planes on the airfield, chanted singsong insults, and banged on metal fuselages. They tried to taunt the Marines into losing their tempers and shooting their rifles, which would reveal the Marines' locations.

At first light, the Japanese slipped back into their tunnels. Angry Marines dug burned and distorted enemy corpses out of pillboxes. They carried the bodies of 120 Marines to the Fifth Division's cemetery near Mount Suribachi. By then, 1,000 Marines had lost their lives on Iwo Jima. No one knew how many Japanese had died.

Then the Third Marine Division moved into the position between the Fifth and Fourth divisions. The drive for Airfield #2 began.

The rain continued, making everyone even more miserable. The Fifth gained 400 yards but suffered severe casualties. Nine officers, many of them Jack's friends, died that day.

The Marines ran out of sand. That night, Fifth Marines built their foxholes out of rocks. Cold and hungry, they drank cold water and gnawed on hard biscuits out of their K rations. No hot stew, no hot coffee. During the night, the rain stopped.

Around midmorning, Jack saw an amazing sight. Flying from the topmost peak of Mount Suribachi was the American flag.

That morning, the Twenty-eighth Regiment had gotten no farther than the base of the mountain. But then a platoon had started up the ashy, rocky northeast slope. Hundreds of outraged Japanese rained crushing fire down on them. The Marines scrambled ever upward. They skirted rocks, bypassed caves, ran when they could, and crawled when they couldn't run.

A sailor, observing the action from a ship, said: "Those gyrenes ought to get flight pay."

Around 1000, a four-man patrol led by Sgt. Sherman B. Watson, reached the volcano's lip. Then another patrol joined them. With them was a Navy medic who had just tagged along. Machine guns littered the ground.

Scouting around the enemy's water system, the squad found a pipe with a hole shot through it. They ran a rope through the hole and lashed the Stars and Stripes to the pipe. Six of them planted the flag in soft ground on the north rim of the crater.

The island went wild. A Navy beachmaster turned up the volume on his public address system and announced the raising of the flag. Sailors rang ships' bells; they blew whistles and foghorns.

Field radios spread the word: "The American flag flies over Suribachi." Everyone turned to look. Men under fire crawled out of their foxholes. Tens of thousands of Marines and sailors and soldiers stood and stared. They pointed. They shouted, "The flag's up." Some wept; others cheered. They pounded each other's backs. To the exhausted, bearded, filth-encrusted men, the flag signified the battle's greatest victory to date.

Jack gave a Texas "yahoo." He hollered as loud as if he were back at Baylor yelling for a touchdown.

Two hours later, the Marines found a 20-foot pipe and replaced the flag by one twice as big. The new flag was large enough for the Japanese to see, too. The entire world soon saw the picture snapped by Associated Press photographer Joe Rosenthal. Rosenthal's photo won the Pulitzer prize. It also lulled many Americans into believing that Iwo Jima was ours. A grave error. The battle would rage another month; another 5,000 men would die.

Meanwhile, all three divisions went back to fighting with renewed courage. But they bucked ever-worsening resistance. A unit bedded down in its foxholes one night, only 30 yards from where it started out that morning. Another platoon took the same hill four times before managing to hang on to it.

Too, the Marines were up against General Kuribayashi's cunning defenses. He had situated Airfield #2 amid hundreds of pillboxes, arranged to fire straight down the runway.

The Fourth Division had not moved for three days. They butted up against treacherous Hill 382, so named because it was 382 feet above sea level. The hill bristled with concrete pillboxes that faced three directions.

The Third Division was unable to advance up the center of Airfield #2. The distance between the two landing fields was one mile, but it seemed like a thousand to the Third. Japanese fired from every cave and fissure, from every rock and mound of dirt. The enemy had seeded the ground with so many land mines that American demolitions squads couldn't mark them.

The Fifth advanced rapidly along the west coast, but they had to pull up at the southern end of Airfield #2. There they waited for the Third to catch up. There could not be such a wide gap in the lines.

To break the impasse, the Marines massed all their shock weapons in one sector just north of the first airfield. Backed up by the Navy's heavy guns and fighter planes, they blasted the enemy-held area. Commanders of all three divisions placed their tank crews under the Fifth Division's tank commander. Ten tanks ground forward. Six tanks struck land mines. More tanks followed. A medium tank clattered to within 50 feet of a pillbox and blasted its aperture with round after round of 75mm shells. Grenades flew at the tank like hornets. Then a Japanese soldier, clad only in a G-string and clutching a hand grenade, ran out and threw himself in front of the tank's tread. He was a fanatic kin to *kamikaze* pilots, fighting under the Japanese code of *bushido*. No surrender. The

Marines heard a muffled "whap" as the grenade exploded. Still firing, the tank lurched on. It rolled over the martyr's body.

A dozen tanks forced passageway along the edge of a bluff and lumbered down a taxi strip linking the two airfields. When they reached the fringes of Airfield #2, Marine riflemen ran beside them up the north-south runway. They crossed the strip and raced for the 50-foot ridge opposite the junction. They plunged into the middle of a hostile group of Japanese troops. For a time, Marines and Japanese battled each other with rifle butts, Kabar knives, and bayonets. Then the Marines picked up their wounded and fell back.

An hour later, the rest of the Third Division reached the southern edge of the east-west runway. That maneuver ruptured the enemy's main defense lines. The Third pulled into position and moved abreast of the Fifth, erasing the gap in the front lines.

At last, the Fifth Division advanced. They hacked out a 200-yard gain, then another 300. A platoon lieutenant led his men 450 yards down the beach. Near a sulfur blowhole, they came to a squad of Japanese. The platoon took a prisoner. The prisoner and his companions had sneaked through Marine lines all the way from Suribachi. Traveling mostly underground, they had been trying to reach other units in the north.

A pillbox halted the Marines. They found themselves short of TNT, dynamite, mortar ammunition, tanks, trucks—everything. Down on the beach a weapons crew dismantled a howitzer and carried it in sections up to the front. They reassembled the weapon and wiped out the pillbox.

Then Easy and Fox companies moved up beside the Twenty-sixth Regiment for the big push. They entered a barren plateau. It was a terrain of craggy hills and cliffs, twisting ravines and gullies, crumbling boulders and struggling brushwood.

The Marines began to swing north onto broken rocky ground. Easy advanced 50 yards; Fox pushed three hundred more. Suddenly, the Twenty-seventh halted when its lead squads came to an open sandy valley. The Marines called it "Death Valley," for it teemed with cement-lined blockhouses buried six feet deep. Loopholes cut in the walls accommodated 81mm mortars. Stone slabs or boards partially covered the roofs. Soil on top was planted with grass and bushes. From the air, American pilots could not distinguish the bunkers from the surrounding scrubland.

Marine leaders called for a bombardment of the valley.

By then, with phone lines strung, Jack Lummus took on a new duty. From a rise near Suribachi, he and a naval liaison officer spotted targets. Jack radioed Colonel Wornham's command post where to direct ground artillery fire. The Navy man notified ships and bomber pilots.

"Tell them to fire on the southwest edge of 163 and the southeast edge of 164," one of them would say. The numbers referred to keyed blocks on aerial maps. Within 10 minutes or less, shells rained down.

Jack called in coordinates to bombard "Death Valley." When the shelling ceased, Fox Company was ordered into the valley to help another unit. They would have to cross the valley and dig in before dark. To do so, the company had to make its move at least two hours before sunset.

Company F ran down the slope, screaming and shooting at anything that resembled a target. The deep valley was alive with targets, all firing back. The most obvious targets, however, were the 200 Marines themselves. They had plunged headlong into a trap.

Japanese blasted the intruders with everything they had. From the front, they fired their vicious Nambu machine guns. From undergrowth on the left, they lobbed mortar shells. Knee mortars whirred through the air. The Japanese strapped the crude two-inch firing mechanisms to their legs. Stopping and propping their knee on a rock, they aimed and fired.

More Japanese guarded the island's northern approaches from a steep, jagged rocky ridge. Aiming their artillery down on the valley, they fired point-blank at any Marine who walked into their sights. Prime targets were Marines carrying flame-throwers or radios with raised antennas.

The Marines suffered heavy casualties. Company E joined the attack and quickly lost 16 men in a mortar barrage. Lt. Frank Fitch, the second to command Easy Company since D-Day, was wounded. Fox Company's commander, Capt. Donald H. O'Rourke, also was wounded. Jack's fishing buddy, First Lt. Richard

Tilghman, took his place. In 10 minutes, 40 men of Fox Company's 200 were wounded or killed.

Fox Company charged another 200 yards, then smacked up against the first pillboxes of the enemy's massive cross-island defense line.

"We were pinned down," recalled Don Hamilton. "All we had to defend ourselves with was rifles. No machine guns got up to our line. We were all waiting for someone to advise moving back." At last, a tank driven by a platoon sergeant blasted through to the far side of the valley. The Marines withdrew to a better position.

Then the Fifth Division dropped back to the rear for a day of rest. When they trudged 100 yards behind the front, Jack didn't recognize them. Boys who had been under his command for several months shuffled along like old men. Under week-old beards and soot-smudged cheeks, faces were lined and pinched. Bloodshot, watery eyes held a blank stare. Through puffy, blue-gray lips, they gasped as though trying to suck in fresh air. Their hands were black and stiff from tossing "pineapples," or hand grenades, from firing rifles and BARs. Most had lost so much weight that their fatigues drooped from hunched shoulders. Their ragged and torn dungarees, encrusted with dirt, gaped where buttons had been ripped off. These were the "raggedy ass Marines."

Behind the retreating Marines, the Japanese also pulled back. The pause allowed Marines time to look around. Along the main defense network, they found a tunnel 800 yards long. Pillboxes bristling with machine guns occupied each of its 14 entrances. Marines located bunkers with 220mm mortars—bigger than the Navy's eight-inch guns—and hundreds of rockets nine feet long, nine inches in diameter. They examined the enemy's spigot mortars. Between five and 16 feet long and one to two feet in diameter, the mortars tumbled through the sky like huge trash cans. They weren't accurate, but if they did land on a target, they exploded into long steel rods.

The recess also allowed General Rockey to assess the damages. He must have groaned when he saw the casualty list. After six days of fighting, 9,000 Marines were reported wounded, missing, or killed. He may have taken some comfort from knowing that 50,000 Marines were on the island by then.

Those who had survived Death Valley slept as if dead that night. They didn't waken even when Marine artillery and destroyer shells smashed a large group of Japanese trying to sneak down the west coast. In bright moonlight, a desperately thirsty enemy was trying to broach the Twenty-seventh's lines. They came to recapture the two water wells the Fifth Division had overrun the day before. By then, all of Kuribayashi's wells were behind American lines. The Japanese were forced to rely on rainwater.

It seemed eerily quiet the next morning, February 25, when a jeep drove up and tossed out sacks of mail. For the first time since the Fifth Division left Hawaii, nearly three months earlier, a mail ship had caught up with them. A plane from the Marianas dropped down on Airfield #1's north-south runway. It carried mail for all the Marines.

Jack went off by himself to read his letters. He read worried letters from his mother and sisters. And then he found some of the letters I had written from Glendale, California.

A day or two later, the mail plane took off for Saipan. It carried 100,000 Victory-mail letters from the men on Iwo. Cameras on the plane reduced V-mail letters to microfilm, the only way such a volume of mail could be transported. When the films arrived in the States, the negatives were developed. Individual one-page letters were printed on paper about the size of a five by seven photograph.

One of those V-mails was addressed to me. Jack's letter dated February 25 wasn't delivered to my house for a few weeks. By then, the Marines had left Iwo Jima and returned to Hawaii. In his letter, Jack assured me he was safe. "I'm okay," he wrote. I believed with all my heart that Jack had survived his first battle.

Hearing from Jack also told me that the letters I had resumed writing had reached him. It meant the end of the strain I had imposed between us.

But the war wasn't over. After Jack and the other Marines posted their letters, they cleaned their gear and stocked up on ammunition and K rations. Leaders reorganized their devastated units and conscripted replacements among the Marines working behind the lines.

The next morning, the Fifth Division headed north again. The Second Battalion, under heavy fire, scrambled along a cliff that bordered the western edge of Airfield #2.

By noon, they had reached the front lines. Overhead, the skies roared with the noise of dive bombers and exploding mortar. Under their feet, the earth shook with concussions. It was impossible to single out individual sounds in an atmosphere so saturated with noise that it threatened to crush one's skull.

The Second scurried past Death Valley. They topped a ridge and looked down on another valley, one just as threatening. Japanese opened fire from caves along the ridge, pinning down the Second's right flank.

The Marines' call for air support nearly turned into disaster. To signify their position for the bomber pilots, the Marines marked their forward margins with white strips of cloth and colored smoke. Japanese sneaked out and stole the cloth panels. For 90 minutes, the Second found itself under fire from their own bombers. They cleared up the mistake and advanced again.

By mid-afternoon, the Second dug foxholes and waited for other units to catch up. The Third Division advanced, plunging the Twenty-sixth Regiment into the midst of enemy lines. The Japanese were forced out. All the Marines yelled and cheered when they spotted the enemy out in the open, retreating. That was a rare sight on Iwo Jima.

That evening, Fifth Division tanks blundered onto a contingent of 500 Japanese cooking rice. American tanks blasted the supper crowd with every weapon they had. The survivors ran off.

The Fifth still had a long way to go. Three-fifths of the

island remained to be conquered.

When the sky lightened the next morning, Marines saw, 800 yards ahead, the ugly slopes of a hill. The armament on Hill 362A was key to the enemy's defense of northern Iwo. It was the Second's next target.

Fierce shellfire poured down from the hill. Caves, blockhouses, and concrete pillboxes dotted its jagged, rocky outcroppings and vertical cliffs. The terrain was too rough for tanks and too uneven for artillerymen to set up their 37mm weapons. And it was too far away for Jack and his naval officer to direct artillery or air fire. The only help the Marines got was from flame-thrower and demolitions teams.

A halftrack finally lurched up and demolished a pillbox, and the Fifth moved 500 yards up the beach. They dug in on top of a rocky ridge. Then their flanks and rear came under heavy fire, and they had to retreat. When the Marines retook the ridge the next morning, they found another Marine. Alone and wounded and cold, he had survived the night.

Then help came from a different source. Two spotter planes landed at the first airfield. Because their engines sounded like washing machines, Marines nicknamed them "grasshoppers" or "Maytag washers." The pilots began to fly over the front, spotting targets for the artillery and radio-equipped jeeps. Eleven more spotter planes landed, and Marines rigged them with bazookas, rockets, and bombs. Those pilots flew low over enemy lines, searching out targets. Then 28 fighter planes came to strafe, drop napalm, and bomb enemy rocket-launching sites. Navy search planes arrived to hunt submarines.

The tide turned, and the Third Division broke through to Motoyama Plateau. Now it was the turn of the Fifth and Fourth divisions to catch up.

A heated argument broke out between Marine commanders and Vice Adm. Richmond Turner. The Marines wanted to bring the rest of the Third Division's troops ashore. Admiral Turner insisted there were enough Marines on Iwo. Riflemen up at the front would have put up an argument about that. Nor did they like it when the fleet pulled up anchor and sailed to Okinawa.

Meanwhile, the Twenty-seventh's Second Battalion left the front for a rest again. This time they plodded back to the base of Mount Suribachi.

The Fifth's area at the rear resembled a small military city. Jammed with men and machines, it buzzed with activity. All available vehicles dragged sledges loaded with equipment and ammunition to the open-air warehouses the Seabees had built. There were ammunition dumps, the Fifth Division's hospital with its underground wards and operating rooms, and the Fifth Division's cemetery. Engineers had driven pipes into a natural spring, and Marines could take hot showers. They had also installed a water distillation unit.

There was even a galley. From pots set on tables, messboys dished up fried Spam and scrambled powdered eggs. And coffee. It was instant coffee, but it was brown and hot.

Exhausted Marines back from the front awoke around midnight when the Japanese started firing their heavy weapons. Some shells soared harmlessly over Suribachi and splashed into the ocean. Others hit supply dumps, vehicles, artillery, and foxholes with sleeping Marines in them. Jack heard the massive explosions when the shell hit the Fifth Division's main ammunition dump. The dump caught fire and its blaze lit up the southern half of the island. Flares skyrocketed; rifle bullets crackled; mortar shells exploded; artillery projectiles flew.

Marines jumped out of their foxholes and raced to the dump. The Fifth's service troops, ignoring the danger, ran into the flames, rescuing shells. Jack and others pitched in to help, running into the flames again and again.

Air raid alarms and poison-gas alarms went off. A burning 105mm shell exploded, setting telephone wires on fire, knocking out communications to artillery units. Finally, bulldozer drivers shoved sand over the dump. By 0700 the next morning, the flames were smothered, and the fire was under control. But one-fourth of the Fifth Division's ammunition had gone up in flames.

Don Hamilton missed the excitement. He had fainted when Fox Company first arrived at the rear area. Doctors diagnosed his severe dysentery and sent him out to a hospital ship.

William Eslinger didn't miss it. He got hit by shrapnel. After being treated at a first aid tent, he went back to his duties as Second Battalion's chief clerk typist. One of his jobs would be to type Jack Lummus' résumé. It would accompany Major Antonelli's recommendation that Jack be promoted to captain.

CHAPTER TWENTY-ONE

A HERO DIES

On the morning of March 6, 1945, Jack Lummus was summoned to battalion headquarters. He found Major Antonelli waiting for him.

"Jack, I want you to take over the third rifle platoon," the major said. The platoon was on the front line, heading the northward advance. But their lieutenant had broken under the strain of battle—battle fatigue—and had left the platoon to flounder without anyone to lead them.

Jack trudged toward the front. It was about 200 yards, a short walk if he'd been strolling through bluebonnets on the Texas prairie. But slogging through the war-damaged terrain of Iwo Jima, it took him more than an hour to get there. The way was clogged with disabled tanks and wrecked artillery pieces. He zigzagged around shell holes in which hundreds of Marines sought shelter from gunfire.

Some were sprawled, asleep; others squatted, writing letters or cleaning and reloading their rifles.

The fight to oust the Japanese from Iwo Jima had been going on for 15 days, and Jack couldn't remember ever being quite so exhausted. His boots felt heavy as if someone had poured concrete into the soles. He struggled to lift one foot in front of the other. He smelled like a rotten egg, too. Five days earlier, he had rinsed off in a crude outdoor shower. Already his face and hands and dungarees looked gray from the fine film of volcanic dust that coated them.

The men he would be taking charge of, though, probably would be 10 times worse off than he was. While he had been at the other end of the island, directing artillery fire, they had spent most of their time at the battlefront.

Jack figured he'd know some of the men. He'd played touch football with some of them on Hawaii and back at Camp Pendleton. Many would be strangers, though. There had been so many casualties during the past two weeks. Most of these boys would be replacements, right off the boat from boot camp. He hoped not, for they all had a tough assignment ahead. He preferred to work with seasoned Marines.

He rounded a jagged boulder and heard the loudest uproar he'd ever heard. The racket was noisier than the crowd at any Texas-Oklahoma football game. He had to be nearing the front.

He skirted other boulders and dodged in and out of foxholes. Finally, he located the platoon, or what was left

of it. Certainly there weren't all 40 of the men who made
up a platoon. The rest had either been wounded and
carried back to a hospital ship. Some, of course, had
been killed.

The men who remained crouched in holes. They
called them foxholes, but infantrymen dug foxholes with
shovels. On this part of the island, the terrain consisted of
hard rock. There was no dirt to shovel. The explosion of
huge shells had blasted these holes. Some of those shells
had been lobbed off the ships' decks. The Marines' gigantic cannons at the other end of the island had made most
of the holes.

Jack walked up to each hole, checking the men.
Volcanic ash had coated their faces a ghostly gray. Strain
had etched boys' faces with deep lines. They resembled
old men. At the same time, they looked like a bunch of
scared kids, cowering in the holes, shoulders hunched
over their weapons. They had reason to be afraid. Enemy
riflemen, perched high among the huge rocks and ridges
up ahead, showered bullets down on them.

"Get that platoon through that gorge," Major Antonelli
had ordered. He expected Jack and his men to pry the
Japanese off those ridges and chase them clear off the end
of the island. Not far from Jack's platoon waited General
Kuribayashi and what were left of his 23,000 Japanese soldiers. They had burrowed into an indestructible underground blockhouse. From that position, the wily general
waited for the Marines. From there, he intended to fight
his last battle. He vowed to defend his headquarters until

his weapons held no more bullets, until he had no more soldiers to command, until his own body held no more breath. He would neither surrender nor make it easy for the Americans to defeat him. He would fight to the death.

Antonelli wasn't here, and Jack wondered what the major's orders would be were he in charge of this platoon. These youngsters were demoralized and frightened. They were also out of everything: ammunition, food, water. More than anything else, they especially lacked courage. Jack couldn't just force them to advance against the barrage of deadly rifle fire and hand grenades that rained down on them.

Jack located the stash of ammunition and weapons. He started to move up and down the line, making sure his men had grenades and bullets. "How y'all doing?" he'd ask. If a man's rifle jammed, Jack would toss it behind the lines and give him another.

One boy wanted to talk about the lieutenant Jack had replaced.

"Combat affects a lot of us—officers as well as enlisted men," Jack said. "Some guys can't handle the noise. Or they can't stand to see their buddies get shot." He patted the Marine on the shoulder. "That's why I came up here with you. We'll get things shaped up. Before you know it, we'll run the Japs off those rocks and chase 'em to the end of the island." Jack left the Marine feeling better.

About midmorning, Corporal Don Hamilton came along and saw Jack relocating his machine gun squad. Jack recognized Hamilton as one of the noncoms under him when he commanded Fox Company. "Hey, Red," Jack hollered at Hamilton, "you look like you just stepped out of a barber shop."

Hamilton explained that he'd passed out from dysentery, and the medics had sent him to a hospital ship. When he regained consciousness, he had smelled so bad the sailors stuck him under a shower and gave him clean dungarees to wear. They issued him a new Browning Automatic Rifle, put him on a gig, and sent him back.

"I'm trying to find Fox Company," Hamilton said.

"They're next door." Jack pointed to his right. "But, look, pardner, why don't you stick around for a while? I need you and that shiny BAR to guard my back while I whip this platoon back into shape."

For the rest of the morning, Hamilton scrambled along behind Jack as he strode up and down the lines. Everyone else was running in a crouch, but Jack stood upright, straight and tall. He ignored the snipers firing down from the ridges. About noon, Jack thanked the corporal, shook his hand, and sent him on his way.

While Jack was busy reorganizing his platoon, the enemy had inched closer. Now they occupied pillboxes on the floor of the gorge. They fired from caves on the walls of the ridges and the one-man foxholes called "spider traps." They bombarded the Marines' foxholes with bullets and grenades. Other Japanese flung grenades over the top of the ridges. Jack and his men threw grenades back. At one point, Jack ran out of grenades and pitched rocks at the enemy.

The Japanese kept the Marines under constant barrage. Exploding ammunition thundered all around, so loud the men couldn't hear Jack's voice when he yelled at them. If he needed to give an order to a squad leader, he tossed a handful of pebbles. The startled man would look around to see Jack giving him hand signals. If Jack wanted a machine gun relocated off to the right, he threw stones at the gunner. When he got his attention, he pointed out where he wanted him to move.

With the enemy holding the sides and ridges of the ravine, Jack couldn't send his men through the gorge. Japanese snipers would pick off every Marine that started through. It would be a turkey shoot.

The battle went on for a day and a night and half of another day. Thirty-six hours. On the morning of March 8, 1945, Jack knew he had to break the impasse. He got Major Antonelli on the field telephone. "Send me tanks, Tony," he yelled. "I need tanks."

Later, the radio man ran up to Jack. "The major's on the radio. He says the tanks got up to battalion headquarters, but the terrain's too rough. They can't get through to us."

Jack took Keith Neilson and two or three others back to bring the tanks forward. When Thomas Bruns, captain of the tank company, saw Jack run up, he realized how badly Jack needed the big Shermans' help. Jack didn't waste time picking up the phone on the outside of the tank to communicate with the driver. Instead, if he wanted the tank to move forward or turn, he pounded the butt of his rifle on the tank's hull.

Guided by Jack and his squad, the tanks rolled through an almost constant volley of mortar and rifle fire. They reached the beleaguered platoon's position. Jack ran from one group of his men to the other.

"Come on, let's get going," he ordered. "We'll follow the tanks through the gorge."

At a signal from Jack, the tanks started rolling. The men in the platoon ran alongside. The bulk of the tanks would shield them from enemy fire.

Bruns' tanks advanced about 100 yards, rumbling past pillboxes, foxholes, and spider traps. Enraged Japanese unleashed a great, bitter volume of rifle fire, and the men running beside the tanks had to turn back.

When Bruns reached the other side of the ravine, he turned his tanks around. He planned for the Shermans to fire heavy shells at enemy snipers. If he forced them off the ridges, Jack could lead his Marines through the gorge.

But then a horrified Bruns saw that the enemy had stopped Jack's platoon. At ranges of less than 15 or 20 feet, Marines and Japanese heaved grenades at each other.

"Hold your fire," Bruns yelled into his intercom. The tanks sat on the opposite side of the battlefield. It would be impossible for Bruns to fire without hitting Jack and his Marines. The captain sat in his tank, helpless and frustrated, watching a horrible scenario unfold.

A sudden burst of rifle fire erupted from a pillbox built into the rocks. The Marines disappeared into foxholes. Everyone but Jack, that is.

Bruns saw the tall, lanky form of Jack Lummus appear. Jack carried his carbine in one hand and a grenade in the other. The pockets of his dungarees bulged with more grenades. He ran like a mountain lion to a large rock a few yards from the ugly steel pillbox. He crouched by the rock, out of sight from the bunker's opening. Recovering from their shock, snipers in other pillboxes and the caves and crevices leveled their rifles at the lofty American. Bullets zinged around him.

Jack wrapped his big hand around one of the grenades and wrenched out the safety pin. He jumped to his feet and sprinted the last distance to the pillbox's opening. He flopped against its armored side. With a quick flick of his wrist, he flung the grenade inside. He sprang back and hugged the wall. He stood there, waiting. Bullets ricocheted. Then the ground jumped. Smoke spurted out of the pillbox's mouth. There was a muffled crash. Jack ran to the front again and fired his carbine into the smoke-filled cavern.

Whirling around, Jack raced toward the lines. An enemy soldier threw a hand grenade. It landed nearby and exploded, knocking Jack flat. He got up, sort of shook himself, and started running again.

Still being fired on by an angry enemy, Jack reached the platoon. He strode up and down.

"Come on out, let's move forward now."

He motioned to Bruns, pointing out other obstacles for his tanks to fire on.

The men started to climb out of their shellholes. Then

another pillbox started firing at them. Jack ran toward it. But another grenade, a lucky pitch by a Japanese, landed on Jack's shoulder. It rolled off and exploded, knocking him down. This grenade injured his shoulder. He scrambled to his feet, ignoring the injury. Why not? He had always ignored a broken nose or a sprained ankle during the heat of a football game.

He raced on to the pillbox. Again the amazed Japanese fired at him. He ran fast—as fast or faster than he'd ever run for home plate. Again the men in the platoon heard a sudden dull discharge. Rock fragments flew over their heads and "pinged" against their helmets. They saw a column of smoke rise from a blockhouse they hadn't seen before.

Jack was out in front again, waving his carbine, yelling. "Let's go, let's go." The men of the third platoon hurried to him. They started through the ravine.

Then the enemy in a third pillbox opened fire. The platoon scurried for cover.

Again, Jack moved out into the open and rushed the emplacement. He edged around it and lobbed in a hand grenade. As before, he ran back to his men.

"Come on, let's dig the Japs out of their holes," he ordered.

Before they started through the gorge this time, Jack and his men scoured the area. They fired carbines into spider holes and crevices; they tossed grenades into caves. Jack came up to Harold Pedersen and asked him to move his heavy machine gun to a new location.

"Watch where you step, lieutenant," Pedersen cautioned as Jack turned to leave. "When we left the rear area, they told us to watch for land mines. I guess the Japs sowed them around like so much bluegrass seed."

"I thought they were all marked," Jack said.

"Some are, some aren't. They use those plastic-detonated mines that you can't pick up on a metal detector."

A short time later, Bruns watched Jack walk away from a foxhole. Suddenly, there was a powerful explosion, and flying rocks and dirt obscured the place where he'd been. When the dust cleared, Bruns saw Jack. He seemed to be struggling to stand up.

Several men ran to him. They knew right away that their lieutenant had been severely injured. Tears rolled down the cheeks of strong Marines, men who had already seen too much death and tragedy.

Wayne Dust, who had played many touch football games with Jack, knew it was imperative that they get their lieutenant to the hospital tent immediately. He left to find a medic or a stretcher.

Keith Neilson lay down on the ground beside Jack, comforting him until help arrived.

"Well, did we take the ridge? Did we reach our goal?" Jack asked.

"Yes, lieutenant," Neilson replied, "we got where you wanted us to go."

Jack lay quietly for a moment. In one hand, he gripped the baseball cap he'd worn under his helmet. Then he said, "I won't play any more football."

"No," Neilson answered.

Dust hurried up. He couldn't find a corpsman but he'd brought a poncho to carry Jack on.

Four of the men carried Jack toward the first aid tent, 200 yards to the rear. As they passed familiar faces, Jack told his men, "Keep going, keep going."

Someone laid a blanket over Jack's lower body, but Dust had already seen the severe damage to Jack's legs. Would Jack... would his lieutenant with that huge, burning desire to win... would he want to live with his legs in that condition?

They reached the first aid station and laid Jack on the ground. Marines came from all over. They gathered around Jack.

"How do you feel?" one of the men asked.

"Fine," Jack answered, "except my legs sure hurt."

Jack's face was as gray as the ground he lay on. His eyelids fluttered slightly, and an enormous pool of blood surrounded the poncho.

A Marine offered Jack a sip of brandy from one of the small bottles they all carried.

"Thanks a lot," Jack said, "but you better keep it. Looks like I'll be going home soon. You'll need it worse than I do."

Dr. Thomas Brown was in charge of the first aid tent. He was also Jack's good friend and admired Jack's athletic abilities.

He examined Jack and winced. The graceful body of his friend, only 29 years old, so badly mutilated. Like

Dust, he wondered if Jack would care to live with his legs in such deplorable condition.

Jack, still crushing his baseball cap in his hand, looked up at the doctor and grinned. "Well, Doc, looks like the New York Giants lost a mighty good end today," he said.

Dr. Brown knew how urgent it was that he send Jack on to the Fifth Division's hospital tent where they had better medical equipment. He squatted beside Jack, getting him ready to withstand the four-mile transfer.

Major Antonelli ran up. "No more games, Tony," Jack said. "A guy with no legs cain't run." It occurred to Dr. Brown that Jack had pulled strength from an enormous reservoir inside his soul. He spent it to comfort his friends.

Dr. Brown administered blood plasma and tied on combat dressings. He sent Jack on his way. There weren't any jeep ambulances in the vicinity, so Wayne Dust and a radioman carried Jack's stretcher.

"I'm all right, I'm all right," Jack told his friends as he left. "Don't worry about me."

An ambulance met the trio halfway. Dust helped load Jack in. "He was still gripping his baseball cap in his hand," Dust said, "and clenching his arms and his shoulders. He was talking a blue streak, but talking rationally."

At the hospital tent, two Navy doctors tended Jack. They were Lieutenants Graham Evans and Howard Stackhouse, Jr. Dr. Stackhouse, who came from Houston, had met Jack on one of the ships that had brought them to Iwo Jima.

The doctor lifted the blanket. He assessed Jack's injuries and realized Jack wouldn't live long. He felt that Jack knew it, too.

Jack looked down at his legs. "Doc, as one good Texan to another, looks like you're going to have to do a little trimming on me," he whispered.

In desperation, although he knew it would be futile, Dr. Stackhouse took Jack into the operating room. By then, the doctors thought Jack might survive the injuries to his legs. But he couldn't survive the internal injuries caused by the blast.

The pharmacist furnished Jack with 18 pints of blood that day. Every once in a while, Jack smiled. At one point, he raised himself on an elbow.

Then later that afternoon, Jack looked up at the surgeon and said, "Well, Stack, it looks like the New York Giants have lost a good end."

Maybe it sounds strange for a man in such dire straits to repeat a phrase over and over. But one suffering such a traumatic shock to his system would dwell on his greatest loss.

The doctor and Jack talked for a while. Then Jack asked for a cup of coffee. He took a large swallow and lay his head back down. He smiled. He closed his eyes. He never opened them.

That evening, March 8, 1945, the Marines who knew First Lt. Jack Lummus buried him. His simple grave was located in Plot 5, Row 13, Grave 1244, in the Fifth Division Cemetery at the base of Mount Suribachi.

Decades later, Dr. Thomas Brown wrote a heartfelt eulogy for his friend:

"Thus ended the career of the graceful, lean, drawling, tough 'Cactus Jack' Lummus, football star at Baylor, Marine at Iwo Jima. It was my privilege, my honor, to know and to be physician to Jack. He was never salaried at $1 million per year. He never wore a Super Bowl ring. Of all the hordes of professional football players only he, along with Maurice Britt of Arkansas, was awarded the Congressional Medal of Honor. He has not been inducted into the Pro Football Hall of Fame. He rests in one of greater dimension."

Jack Lummus' mother, Laura, received her son's Medal of Honor in ceremonies at Ennis on Memorial Day, 1946. Rear Admiral J.J. Clark of the U.S. Navy presented the medal to Mrs. Lummus nearly fourteen months after her son's death on Iwo Jima. (*Photograph by* Dallas Times Herald *photographer Johnny Hayes, courtesy Sue Merritt*)

EPILOGUE

The shock of seeing Jack Lummus carried away on a poncho infuriated the Marines of Easy Company's third platoon. They had lost "Cactus Jack," their sports hero and one of their favorite officers. They wanted to avenge his death. They did so by doing exactly what he told them to do. They kept going.

The platoon charged 300 yards through the gorge. That platoon of fewer than 40 Marines blasted and burned more than 100 Japanese from their holes.

The breakthrough incited all Marines in that sector. Other units followed Company E through the gap to a ledge 800 yards forward. It was one of the longest, most successful offensives of the entire Iwo operation. Those angry, determined Marines held that ledge for three days, pinning the enemy in a pocket.

The assault, an American equivalent to a Japanese *banzai* attack, broke the enemy's spirit. Before long, Japanese began to sneak out of their underground

EPILOGUE

fortresses and surrender. They were among the first to surrender.

The Marine Corps attributed the ultimate defeat of the Japanese on Iwo Jima to Company E's triumphant charge. And, the Corps' report continues, the spark that set off this charge was the fatal wounding of "a tremendously popular officer, First Lt. Jack Lummus."

The Iwo Jima campaign didn't end with Jack's death on March 8, 1945. The fighting continued for 18 more days. The battle that admirals and generals estimated would take "a week at the most" lasted more than a month. It had been the Marine Corps' bloodiest World War II battle to date. A total of 5,931 Marines and an additional 890 Seabees, sailors, doctors, medical corpsmen, pilots, and Army men died on the "stinking porkchop."

Iwo was also one of the war's most heroic battles. The president of the United States awarded 27 Medals of Honor to men who fought on Iwo. One Medal of Honor, the nation's highest award, went to Jack Lummus. Forty years later, Jack's sisters christened the M/V *First Lt. Jack Lummus*, one of five U. S. Navy supply ships named for Medal of Honor recipients.

In mid-March, meanwhile, I received the V-mail letter Jack had written two weeks before his death. "I'm okay," he had assured me. The night Jack's letter arrived, Orville Tuttle showed up at my home with two other Marine officers. Why had Jack's friend stopped by? I wondered. He had been with Jack the night we met. Was he now trying to move in on Jack's girl? I didn't know Marine protocol; I didn't know that three Marines often come to notify someone of a loved one's death; I didn't know that Jack had made such an arrangement with Tutt before he shipped overseas. I was so thrilled that I'd heard from Jack, so confident that he would walk away from Iwo Jima. Tutt didn't have the heart to tell me the truth.

A couple of weeks later, I came home for lunch and found my mailbox stuffed with letters I had written Jack. On each envelope was an indelible-ink stamp declaring the letter "Undeliverable, killed in action."

I tried to telephone Jack's family. Instead I reached a woman whose husband collected news clippings about Ennis servicemen. She confirmed that Jack had been killed, but she didn't have any details. Nor did she know how to locate his family. Years later, I went to Hawaii and looked for Jack's grave in the huge Punch Bowl Cemetery. He wasn't buried there. Another time, I drove to Ennis and tried to locate someone from the family. Again, I found myself going down a blind alley. At last, in 1987, I learned the married names of his sisters. I called them and drove to Texas. They greeted me with open arms. I discovered that, at the family's request, the Marine Corps had brought Jack's body back to Ennis.

One sunny August morning, I followed a rock road through Ennis' Myrtle Cemetery. I spotted a small replica of the Medal of Honor next to a flat tombstone. On the granite stone was engraved Jack's name and the dates, October 22, 1915, to March 8, 1945. Once a year, now, I visit the grave. A gnarled old elm tree shades me as I sit there remembering. When I leave, I place a single rose on the grave marker.

I have found Jack again. At last.

The MV 1st Lt. Jack Lummus, flagship of the U.S. Navy's Maritime Prepositioning Squadron Three, was christened on February 22, 1986, by Jack Lummus' sisters, Thelma Wright of Austin, Texas, and Sue Merritt of Fort Worth. The MV Lummus is one of thirteen ships to be built and named after Marine Corps' Medal of Honor recipients. Permanently based at Guam, the MPS ship is operated by civilian crews. It rapidly carries most of the equipment that 1,800 Marines require when responding to threats from America's enemies. The 44,000-ton, 11-story-tall Lummus was one of the first ships to supply troops landing in the Persian Gulf-Desert Storm conflict and the first ship at Somalia. It also fulfilled another duty when it served as a rescue/evacuation ship during the devastating volcanic eruption in the Philippines. (Courtesy American Overseas Marine Corporation)

NO MAN WALKS ALONE

The Marine Corps today attacks enemy held territory much the same as it did during World War II. Of course, more advanced equipment, such as the hovercraft, is used.

When a Marine rifleman first leaves a ship and heads for land, he is convinced that every hostile opponent he faces has a weapon aimed directly at him. But he need not feel alone, for he is surrounded by more "friends" than the eye can see.

The basic makeup of a Marine division is its fighters: the riflemen, machine gunners, flame thrower operators, etc. The numbers of these can be broken down as follows:

Division:	3 regiments of 2,000 men each
Regiment:	3 battalions of 600 men each
Battalion:	3 companies of 200 men each
Company:	3 platoons of 60 men each
Platoon:	3 squads of 15 to 20 men each

By the time a division is fully staffed, however, it will consist of 25,000 men. Also going along in support of the Marine will be:

Air support control
Amphibious transport battalion
Armored amphibious units
Artillery regiment
Howitzer battalion
Amphibious reconnaissance
Bomb disposal
Burial detail
Civil affairs
Dog platoon
Enemy materials and salvage units
Engineer battalions
Evacuation hospital
Field depot
Harbor specialist
Intelligence
Joint assault battalion
Marine observation squad
Medical battalion
Motor transport battalion
Navajo Code Talkers
Pioneer (replacement) battalion
Rocket detachment
Service battalion (cooks, mail clerks, musicians, etc.)
Seabees
Signal battalion

Tank battalions

The Navy brings the Marines to shore, which often entails the support of 485 ships. These ships stay and serve the Marines by resupplying them with ammunition, fuel, spare parts, food, and other supplies.

And waiting offshore somewhere is the Army, ready to come in and occupy the area.

GLOSSARY OF TERMS

AFT — Far point toward the back of a ship; the stern.

AMTRAC — Combat units boarded amphibious tractors, called "amtracs" that, similar to DUKWs, traveled on land or sea.

APO — Army Post Office. Mail for soldiers was directed to a designated number and forwarded to the addressee's overseas location.

ARMY AIR CORPS — Until 1946, the name and status of the United States Army Air Force.

BANDOLEER — Broad ammunition belt worn over one shoulder.

BAR — Browning Automatic Rifle.

BAZOOKA — Long metal tube for aiming and launching armor-piercing rockets. Requires two men to fire. One holds the tubing over his shoulder while the other inserts the shell.

BIVOUAC — Temporary camp with or without shelter.

BOONDOCKERS — Leather ankle-high boots used for marching or hiking through rough boondocks.

BOONDOCKS — Outlying, remote land used for military training maneuvers.

BOOT — Recent recruit to the Navy.

BOW — Front part of a ship, opposite to the stern.

BRIG — Guardhouse or prison on a U. S. warship.

BULKHEAD — Wall or partition of a ship.

BUNK — Shelf-like bed built into or against a wall, as on a ship.

BUSHIDO — Japanese word meaning "no surrender."

CARGO PALLET — Low platform on which ships' commodities are stacked.

CB&Q RAILROAD — The Chicago, Burlington & Quincy Railroad Company, which ran from Chicago to Denver. Now the Burlington Northern.

CHAMBERPOT HELMET — Metal helmet that looks like an upside-down pot. Supposedly deflects most rifle bullets.

CHIT — Letter, note, or voucher.

COMPANIONWAY — Stairway from a ship's deck to cabins or spaces below.

COXSWAIN — Person who steers a boat. Also cockswain.

DAVIT — Pair of curved uprights projecting over the side of a ship for suspending or lowering a small boat.

D.I. — Drill Instructor.

DOG FACE — Nickname for an Army man.

DUKW — Small boat-tractor combination that travels through water or over land. Pronounced "duck."

DUNGAREES — Work clothing made out of coarse cloth.

FLAMETHROWER — Weapon that shoots a stream of burning

liquid, such as oil or gasoline, at enemy troops or positions.

FLOTATION VEST — Inflated life preserver.

FORWARD — Toward the front of a ship.

FOXHOLE — Hole dug in ground as temporary protection for one or two soldiers against enemy gunfire or tanks.

FROGMEN — Commandos who swim to shore from small boats to assess an enemy's strength or check for defense equipment, such as underwater land mines. Resemble frogs because they wear swimming flaps on their feet.

FUSILLADE — Simultaneous or rapid discharge of many firearms.

GALLEY — Ship's kitchen.

G. I. — Equipment or clothing supplied by the government: Government Issue. Also used as a nickname for a soldier.

GIG — Long, light ship's boat, used to ferry a few men from ship to ship or ship to shore.

GUIDON — Flag that identifies a military unit.

GUNNERY — Heavy guns.

GUNNERY SERGEANT — Enlisted man in charge of gunnery squad. He is called "Gunny."

GUNWALES — Upper edge of the side of a boat or ship.

GYRENES — Nickname for Marines, used especially by sailors.

HEAD — Ship's bathroom.

HIGGINS BOAT — Small boat that holds 36 men and has a hinged ramp on one end for troops to debark.

HOLD — Interior of a ship below deck.

HOURS — Time counted from 2400 midnight to 2359 the next midnight. Noon is 1200.

HOWITZER — Short cannon that fires shells in a high trajectory.

JAPS — Derogatory name used during World War II, meaning Japanese.

KABAR — A seven-inch-long knife.

KAMIKAZE — Suicide attack by a Japanese airplane pilot during World War II. The pilot dove his plane into an American ship, dying in the attempt to destroy the ship.

LONGSHOREMAN — Man who works on the waterfront loading or unloading ships.

LUAU — Hawaiian feast, usually with entertainment.

MAE WEST — An inflated life preserver. *See flotation vest.*

MESS — Where a group of sailors or soldiers regularly eat meals.

MESSBOY or MESSMAN — Military personnel who work in a mess.

MILITARY POLICE — Units with police authority over military personnel. Called MPs.

MORGUE — Room or library of back issues, photos, or clippings from a newspaper, magazine, etc.

MORTAR — Short-barreled cannon.

NAPALM — Jellied gas used in flame throwers and bombs.

NFL — National Football League.

NCO — Noncommissioned officer.

NONCOMMISSIONED OFFICER — Enlisted man above private first class and below warrant officer.

PILLBOX — Enclosed gun emplacement made of cement and steel.

PONCHO — Rubber or waterproofed cloak worn as a raincoat.

PORT — Left side of a ship as one faces forward.

QUARTERMASTER — Officer who assigns quarters to troops and provides clothing, equipment, etc.

QUONSET HUT — Prefabricated corrugated metal building. Shaped like a long half of a cylinder resting on its flat surface. First used by the Army in World War II.

SATCHEL CHARGE — Dynamite or TNT in a small bag.

SEABEES — Construction Battalion. Military men who build and defend harbor facilities, airfields, etc. Called "soldiers in sailors' uniforms."

SHELTER HALF — One-man tent.

SHORE PATROL — Naval military unit that polices sailors and Marines. Called SPs.

SICKBAY — Ship's hospital or dispensary.

S.O.S. — International signal of distress. Used by ships, aircraft, etc., to call or appeal for help. In Morse Code or wireless telegraphy, the signal is: ". . . - - - . . .".

SPIDER HOLES — Small, one-man foxholes.

STANCHIONS — Upright bar or beam used as a support.

STARBOARD — Right-hand side of a ship as one faces forward.

STERN — Rear end of a ship or boat.

SUBMARINE NET — Rope net deep enough and strong enough to keep submarines out of a harbor. At Pearl Harbor, the net was 35 feet deep.

SWAB JOCKEY — Nickname for a sailor.

T.N.T. — Trinitrotoluene. High explosive used for blasting, in artillery shells, etc.

U.S.O. — United Service Organizations. Federal agency that

oversees entertainment for troops at military bases.

V FOR VICTORY — A symbol displaying two fingers in a V-shape. Popularized during World War II by Britain's Prime Minister, Winston Churchill.

YARDARM — Either end of a slender rod or pole across a ship's mast that supports a sail.

LIST OF SOURCES

BOOKS

Blakeney, Jane, *Heroes United States Marine Corps* - 1861-1955. United States Marine Corps, 1957.

Moskin, J. Robert, *The U.S. Marine Corps Story.* New York: McGraw-Hill, 1977.

Newcomb, Richard F., *Iwo Jima.* Toronto: Bantam Books, 1982.

Ross, Bill D., *Iwo Jima, Legacy of Valor.* New York: Vintage Books, 1985.

Wells, John Keith, *Iwo Jima.* No city shown: Quality Publications, 1995.

Wheeler, Richard, *Iwo.* New York: Lippincott & Crowell, 1980.

MAGAZINES

Alexander, Col. Joseph H., "The Americans Will Surely Come." *Naval History,* January-February 1995.

Crouch, Roy, *The (Baylor) Round Up.* 1940.

Evans, Norman S., "Baylor Drug, August 1941." *The Baylor Line,* September 1988.

Falk, Jonni, "They Were Giants." *Giants Extra*, July 1994.

"Lummus Memorial Trophy to Honor Former Athlete," *Baylor Report*, January-February 1973.

Gunn, John, "Giant of a Man." *Orange County Register*, July 27, 1986; also released on Associated Press wire August 18, 1986.

Heard, Dow, and James Farley, *The (Baylor) Round Up.* 1941.

Nalty, Bernard C., "The United States Marines on Iwo Jima: The Battle and the Flag Raising." U.S. Marine Corps Headquarters, Historical Division. Government Printing Office, 1970.

Parks, Lt. William Hays, "Baylor's Hero at Iwo Jima." *The Baylor Line*, January-February 1965, 4-6.

Santelli, James S., "A Brief History of the 27th Marines." GPO, 1968.

NEWSPAPERS

Arkansas Gazette. December 25, 1940.

Austin (Texas) American. May 28, 1946.

Brownsville (Texas) Herald. May 20, 1945.

Corpus Christi (Texas) Caller. May 8, 1945.

El Paso Times. May 6, 1945.

Ennis (Texas) Daily News. May 29, 1946, May 26, 1986.

Ennis (Texas) Daily Times. undated.

Fort Worth Star Telegram. May 28, 1946.

New York Times, Sports sections. August 10, 1941 to December 22, 1941.

San Diego Union, morning edition. January 2, 1944.

St. Louis Sporting News Publishing Company, undated.

San Francisco Chronicle. Associated Press release datelined Denver. May 1, 1945.

Tyler (Texas) Telegraph. May 26, 1946.

U.S.A. Today, Sports section. undated 1990.

Waco (Texas) News-Tribune. April 21, 1948, December 1, 1973.

Wichita Falls (Texas) Times. May 31, 1941 to July 3, 1941, May 20, 1945.

UNPUBLISHED MATERIALS

Eslinger, William M., "Autobiography of William M. Eslinger." Undated. Photocopy.

Giniger, Staff Sgt. Henry, and Staff Sgt. Tony Smith, "The Twenty-Seventh Marines in Combat." Undated. Photocopy.

Hamilton, Donovan E., "Memories of Iwo Jima." 1947. Photocopy.

McCormick, Lynn L., "Iwo Jima Revisited." 1983. Photocopy.

Rondero, Peter J., editor, "Men of Iwo." Newsletters for members associated with Fifth Marine Division, Twenty-seventh Regiment, Second Battalion, Company F. 1988-90.

INTERVIEWS

Doolittle, Charles. Interviews with author. Telephone, three times since 1987.

Howell, Jim Lee. Interview with author. Lonoke, Arkansas, April 1987.

Lindberg, Charles, surviving personnel of first Suribachi flag raising. Interview with author, North Dakota Iwo Jima Survivors Association, Bismarck, North Dakota, 1994.

Lummus family members. Interview with author. Austin, Ennis, Fort Worth, and Colleyville, Texas, on at least ten different occasions since 1987.

Neilson, Keith R., Louis Lanier, R.C. Strome, Clyde M. Griffith, William B. Madden, and Don Johnson, Iwo Jima survivors of Fifth Marine Division, Twenty-seventh Regiment, Second Battalion Company E third platoon. Interviews with author, Wichita Falls, Texas, reunion, Iwo Jima Survivors Association of Texas, February 1993.

Nelson, Travis, and Louis Newman. Interview with author. Bryan, Texas, November 18, 1988.

Duncan, Rea, Wayne Dust, Vernon Hammons, Gene Higgins, Pete Piesik, and Jay Rebstock. Interviews with author. Raiders and Paratroopers reunion, Jackson, Mississippi, 1987.

Urdesich, Milo. Interview with author. Telephone, June 10, 1988.

Wimpee, Dr. W. J. Interview with author. Waco, Texas, November 20, 1988

LETTERS

Bainter, Bill, Jack Black, Maurice Britt, Dr. Thomas M. Brown, Jerry Bush, Matt Capobianco, Danny J. Crawford (Head, Reference Section, U.S. Marine Corps History and Museums Division), John A. Daniels, Hugh Delano (*New York Post* sports-writer), Charles Doolittle, Robert H. Dunlap (Medal of Honor recipient, Iwo Jima), Pete Elliott (Pro Football Hall of Fame), William M. Eslinger, George French, Henry Gendreizig, Loy Gilbert, John Gunn, Donovan Hamilton, Hal Harle, Francis Heenan, Joe Horrigan (Pro Football Hall of Fame), Jim Lee Howell (Giants coach), Robert L. Jackson, Ted Johnson, Charles A. Jones, (quoting Col. J. S. Scales), Wellington Mara (President, New York Football Giants), William McCann, Capt. Thom Merrell (American Overseas Marine Corporation), Richard F. Newcomb (author, *Iwo Jima*), Louis Newman, Walter P. O'Malley, Harold Pedersen, Jim Poole (Giants end), Stan Raytinsky, Harold E. Reynolds, William O. Riggsbee, Peter J. Rondero, Sylvia Rosas, (Department of the Navy, Military Sealift Command,) J.T. Shahan, Bobby R. Taylor, Harry L. Tennison, Sen. Richard A. Tilghman, Thomas Turner (Baylor University), Milo Urdesich, Don Vosberg, C.A. Weathered, Cy Williams, Jack Willis, Dr. W. J. Wimpee (Baylor University), Frank Woschitz (National Football League Association), Cy Young, (Iwo Jima Survivors Association of Texas).

PUBLIC DOCUMENTS

National Archives and Records Administration, National
Personnel Records Center, *Staffing Package* containing rec-
ommendations on which Jack Lummus' Medal of Honor
was based, St. Louis, MO.

U. S. Marine Corps Headquarters, Reference Section, History
and Museums Division, *Medal of Honor Citation of 1st Lt.
Jack Lummus,* Washington, D.C.; GPO.

U. S. Marine Corps Headquarters, *Commemorative Namings in
Honor of Marines from the 27th Regiment,* Washington,
D.C.; GPO.

U. S. Marine Corps Headquarters, 1965, *Biography of 1st Lt. Jack
Lummus, USMCR (Dec),* Washington, D.C.; GPO.

U. S. Marine Corps Headquarters, 1946, *Medal of Honor Citation
of 1st Lt. Jack Lummus, USMCR (Dec.),* Washington, D.C.;
GPO.

USS *Highlands* APA 119, Personnel Log of Charles D. Duke,
CGM, Friday, November 17, 1944 to Wednesday, February
28, 1945.

PHOTO ALBUM

D-day. Mount Suribachi in the background.

Landing on the beach at Iwo Jima.

Securing the beach on Iwo Jima.

Flag raising at Mount Suribachi,
February 23, 1945. (See pages 185 and 186)

Sgt. William F. Curry on Mount Suribachi, February 24, 1945. (above left)
Second Engineers' water distillation unit. One canteen of water was
issued each day to each Marine. (above right)

Japanese pillbox.

Injured on the beach ready to be evacuated to the hospital ship. (left)
Hospital ship off Iwo Jima. (right)

Fifth Marine Division Cemetery. Mount Suribachi in the background.

All photographs in the Photo Album are courtesy of the William F. Curry collection with the exception of two photos of the flag raising which are courtesy of the United States Naval Institute.

INDEX